Dedication:

To my family:

Bear ~ thank you for believing, and for knowing that I would "come to believe."

Will ~ your curiosity, fascination with life and its workings, and desire for truth have challenged and inspired me always.

And to James ~ your creativity, pleasing and lovable nature, and desire to succeed encourage me to be the best mother and person that I can be.

I love you all dearly.

Parenting by the Steps

Nan Landis Hochberger

ISBN 0-7414-3969-7

Published by:

INFI∞ITY
PUBLISHING.COM

1094 New DeHaven Street, Suite 100
West Conshohocken, PA 19428-2713
Info@buybooksontheweb.com
www.buybooksontheweb.com
Toll-free (877) BUY BOOK
Local Phone (610) 941-9999
Fax (610) 941-9959

Printed in the United States of America

Printed on Recycled Paper

Published July 2007

Thank you:

God, for my life, my sobriety, my parents and brothers, my husband, and my divine appointment as my boys' mom.

KOP, for inspiration.

Nancy, for creative and literary support.

Pammy, Sheri, and Darlene, for all your many prayers and backrubs, and all of my sisters at MPG, especially Stacia, Patti, Lori, and Valinda, for their love and prayerful support.

Tina, for showing me how to find freedom and joy in life, and Sandie, Scout, Patty, Tracy, Mimi, and Beth for being my sober sisters always.

LLDD/PQ, for being my best friend.

Alan and Fran, for teaching me to be myself.

Acknowledgments

Brief excerpts from the book *Alcoholics Anonymous* and the Twelve Steps are reprinted and adapted with the permission of Alcoholics Anonymous World Services, Inc. (AAWS). Permission to reprint excerpts from the book *Alcoholics Anonymous,* and to reprint and adapt the Twelve Steps, does not mean that AAWS has reviewed or approved the contents of this publication, or that AAWS necessarily agrees with the views expressed herein. A.A. is a program of recovery from alcoholism only – use of the Twelve Steps in connection with programs and activities which are patterned after A.A., but which address other problems, or in any other non-A.A. context, does not imply otherwise.

The Twelve Steps

(in original form, reprinted with permission from AAWS)

1. We admitted we were powerless over alcohol - that our lives had become unmanageable.
2. Came to believe that a Power greater than ourselves could restore us to sanity.
3. Made a decision to turn our will and our lives over to the care of God, *as we understood Him.*
4. Made a searching and fearless moral inventory of ourselves.
5. Admitted to God, to ourselves, and to another human being the exact nature of our wrongs.
6. Were entirely ready to have God remove all these defects of character.
7. Humbly asked Him to remove our shortcomings.
8. Made a list of all persons we had harmed, and became willing to make amends to them all.
9. Made direct amends to such people wherever possible, except when to do so would injure them or others.
10. Continued to take personal inventory and when we were wrong promptly admitted it.
11. Sought through prayer and meditation to improve our conscious contact with God *as we understood Him*, praying only for knowledge of His will for us and the power to carry that out.
12. Having had a spiritual awakening as the result of these steps, we tried to carry this message to alcoholics and to practice these principles in all our affairs.

Contents

Foreword

At this point, I've been a successful parent for eighteen years. I say successful not because both of my boys are relatively healthy, strong, and pursuing life with enthusiasm, but because they have a sense of who they are; they are beginning to be independent from their father and me, and they are trying to follow God to the best of their teenaged understanding and abilities. This looks very different for each of them, but I believe they are in earnest in their quest for His truth and presence. To me, this is the most amazing and wonderful evidence!

I wasn't raised in a particularly religious or God-based environment. In fact, I sometimes think that science was God in our home. My dad's strong intellect, scientific vocation, literary knowledge and edified point of view certainly molded my belief that in order to be a good Landis, one had to be smart, logical, and very well-read. My mom's Upstate New York farming background influenced me to be hardworking, modest and plain: a no-nonsense, don't-put-on-any-airs type of girl.

Imagine the collision of this background with the liberation of a big university and the hippie, free love, sex, drugs, and rock n' roll culture of the late 60s. I never knew where I fit in; I never felt that I belonged anywhere—that is, until I found the magic solution: drugs and alcohol. With a good buzz on, as they say, I could be anyone. I could do anything. It didn't matter that I was faking it, because no one knew, and even if they did, who cared?

Fifteen years, several damaged relationships, a few dented cars, and many demolished brain cells later, I surrendered to a Power greater than myself in a recovery program. This is where I met God. And not gracefully, I might add. I was angry. I was furious and upset and peeved at the God that I didn't believe in. Yes, I know it's an oxymoron. I didn't know how He could have let this miserable, broken, divorced, misspent life happen to ME. And since it was His fault, I kicked and screamed and cried my way through the Twelve Steps and the work that they required.

But somewhere along the line, those same steps saved me. They gave me the gift of surrendering to a God whom I had never really known. Working the steps saved me from the self abuse, but turning to God for all my concerns relieved me of depression, anxiety, loneliness, and the sorrowful abandonment that I had so freely heaped upon my own self for all of those destructive years.

Parenting by the Steps begins about six years after the point at which I began my walk with the steps. As I was in the practice of using the steps to help me through life, I naturally began leaning on them when I needed parenting help. Incorporating the wisdom, guidance and reliance on God that is inherent in the Twelve Steps is a natural transition for those of us who have worked the steps in "anonymous programs" already.

The non-programmed

But what about those of you who haven't been in a program before? Does this book make sense for you? Is the concept of Twelve Steps too foreign? And why do we have to surrender, anyway? Good questions. I hope that you'll read the book and find the answers for yourselves. I believe that the twelve-step way of life is simple. The steps are merely the guide map to assist you in surrendering the illusion of control, opening up to a Higher Power, and discovering who you are as a parent. They are here to help you become the best, most peaceful and loving parent you can be. I hope and pray that your journey is a joyful one.

Part I — Surrender

Your children are not your children.
They are the sons and daughters of Life's longing for itself.
They come through you but not from you,
And though they are with you yet they belong not to you.
~ Kahlil Gibran

Chapter 1

"It's not our job to make our children happy, it's our job to help them become more human."

~ Dr. Haim Ginott

The first step

I am powerless over my child, and his or her life is unmanageable by me.

Does this seem impossible? Isn't it my job to make sure that my child is happy, successful, contented? Aren't I supposed to ensure that she experiences a carefree, joyous childhood? Isn't it important for me to block those powerful forces that gang up on my child to render him sad, angry, defiant, upset, hurt and damaged? Won't making sure that he is happy ensure that he has a happy, successful adulthood?

These are all good questions that most parents struggle with. And the answer to all of them is "no." It is not your job to ensure happiness; in fact, it's an impossibility, which only the arrogance of our humanness endorses. How can you or I make sure that anyone is happy? Are you happy because of what someone else does or says? You may be elated momentarily or excited by something that a friend does for you; certainly, when my son picks a flower and gives it to me, I feel some momentary joy. But here we're looking at happiness as a state of being. You might wish your child to be happy, but you can't make her so. A lollipop makes her happy for a moment, but it won't make her a happy person.

If you look at the origin of any emotional state, it is from within a person. I am happy because I feel happy inside. I am sad because I feel sad. I am angry, rebellious, upset, tired, lonely, stern, grumpy, or joyful, elated, curious, excited, all because of an internal feeling state. If someone else has the power to make me feel happy, then am I giving over my free will to that person? Am I an automaton? Is that person, then, in complete control of my emotions? Certainly not. Someone may influence the way I feel. The child who picked the flower did a pleasing thing. I felt pleased. I enjoy flowers. I felt happy.

We often say: "he makes me happy," when what we really mean is: "I feel happy because I am reacting to something he did." As we say in the 12-step world, happiness is an inside job.

Sarah, a mom I know, said, "I was unhappy as a child. My parents were never around. They had a lot of money and traveled a lot. I was never told I couldn't do anything, and I was a pretty good kid. I didn't do well in school, but no one got mad at me about that. I had everything I wanted—toys, friends, a new car when I was 16, the best private schools. But I was never happy. I wanted my parents there. I had no discipline or structure. Now, I have my own child. Zoey is 8, and she already has lots of problems. She's restless, does poorly in school, and has no self-esteem. I can't say no to her, because I hate to see her upset. So I give her everything." Sarah is determined to make her child happy, but it's not working. Zoey is not a happy child; she's been diagnosed with learning disorders, and she is argumentative and angry with her mother. When telling me this story, I stopped Sarah and asked her: "Who does Zoey remind you of?" This brought immediate tears to the mom—and to me.

I was an unhappy child. But in the generation before

the Vietnam War, the post-depression parents did not emphasize happiness so much. We were told to "put on a smile," to work hard and save money. On more than one occasion, I was admonished that "you can catch more flies with honey than with vinegar." This always left me a bit confused, since I didn't really want to catch any flies, but I was pretty sure it meant that I was to act happy, no matter how I felt on the inside.

This current generation seems to be at the opposite end of the parenting continuum. I'm not sure whether it's the extreme "me-ism" of the generation that grew up in the 60s and 70s or if it's the techno-hyperdrive that's pressuring today's parents to want their kids to FEEL HAPPY NOW! Even though Sarah "had everything," it did not help her to be happy; now, she is perpetuating the cycle by trying it again with Zoey and wishing for a different result. (This is the definition of insanity, by the way, which we'll discuss further in Chapter 2.)

I am powerless...

What does this mean to me, an average parent?

It means that I am not in control. This is the hardest part to accept. I cannot make my child happy, nor can I make him successful, honest, cheerful, brave, thrifty, clean or reverent. (There's a Boy Scout Oath in there somewhere.) I can *influence* him. Numerous studies have shown that my behavior as a person is the model that my child has for his life, and that this is the greatest influence that he receives. If I am a happy, balanced, successful person, my child has a good chance of becoming one too. But it is not (alas) a guarantee. It is a blueprint upon which my child's experiences, environment, and ability to adapt will all write and edit.

If I give up the notion of control over this child's life, what do I have? I have powerlessness. I have the fact that this child has been loaned to me (I believe by God) to

5

nurture, love, care for physically, discipline, and influence the best that I can within the scope of my very human, fallible nature. Powerlessness means the absolute lack of control over the outcome for this child. I cannot decide his fate. Whether you believe in God or another Higher Power, as we say in 12-step programs, that Power is greater than I am and is in charge of this child. I'm powerless over his moods, feelings, thoughts, dreams, prayers, fantasies, and wishes. I'm powerless over his entire internal experience. This is the nature and extent of my powerlessness.

I do have a measure of control over some aspects of my child's life. I can control the food I buy for her to eat, the home I prepare for her to live in, the rules and duties I set down for her to abide by, and the discipline I use if those rules are not adhered to. All of these things I do have control over. But they are essentially things that I can do. They are not related to her. I can set the rule, "be home by 11:00." I can attempt enforcement of the rule: "you're not allowed out on Saturday because you did not come home by 11:00 on Friday." However, I cannot control whether she actually *obeys* the rule. I can only control myself, my reactions, and my decisions. If she disobeys again and goes out on Saturday, I have recourse: I can sit down with her and reason out a system of behavior that will ensure compliance, I can call the police because she's "run away," and I can ignore her behavior and hope for the best. All of these options are within my control, but how she responds to them is utterly out of my power. I am powerless over my daughter.

Jilly is a 14-year-old young woman in one of my teen groups. She is there because her parents feel that they are unable to control her. She has tried several types of drugs, and uses whatever instruments she can find to cut her arms and legs in small but indiscreet injuries. When asked to stop, she says she has. "I haven't cut myself in a week," is her ready defense. Despite the therapy group she's in, and the fact that she's signed a "no injury" contract with her therapist, at the next sign of distress or anxiety, Jilly will find a pen or a paper clip or whatever is nearby with a sharp edge and re-injure herself. Her need for self-injury (and, I believe, self-control) outweighs her willingness to be contained by the efforts of her parents, school counselors, and therapists. Jilly's parents are, of course, distraught by this, and continually ask: "What did we do?" There is no simple answer for this, and I think it is an irrelevant question. Better to ask: "what do we do now?" The answer to this is not an easy one. Let's start with the first step. You are powerless over Jilly's cutting, and…

…her life is unmanageable by me.

What can you manage in a child's life? When they're little, you can organize their soccer schedule, take them to the shoe store to buy them a sensible pair of shoes, and watch over their homework to lovingly make corrections. You can even cook nutritious and healthful foods to help manage their body's growth. You can manage aspects of their physical, mental and social lives.

But can you manage a tantrumming 3-year-old? Can you manage a surly teenager? What about Jilly? Can you control her need to harm herself? How can you do that? You could hire a guard to follow her around every day and protect her, but even then, you probably wouldn't want to have someone be right next to her in the bathroom or shower. You wouldn't take away all of her dignity and privacy, would you?

When my son Will was in third grade, Mrs. Adams was his strict but loving teacher. He was always trying to please her, and rarely came home with any reports of trouble. One day, he got in the car after school and was uncharacteristically quiet. "How was school?" I cheerfully asked. I got a snarly reply:

"Bad," he said, folding his arms over his chest. "Mrs. Adams yelled at me in front of everyone at the playground line-up."

7

"Oh, no," I replied, alarmed. "You must have been embarrassed!"

"No!" he said, vehemently. "I was pissed off!" Shocked, I remained silent as we pulled into our driveway. He got out of the car, grabbed his green Power Ranger backpack, and stormed into the house. Instantly, I wanted to chase after him and find out what happened. Everything in me wanted to know what he had done, why Mrs. Adams yelled, what happened after that, etc. I was a burning, seething coal of control and management. Tell me! I'll fix it! I wanted to scream.

"Fixing it" for my son has some drawbacks. If I fix this small, third-grade error in judgment or communication or whatever it was, how will he learn to find solutions for himself? How will he learn to make things right when he's in trouble? He'll come to me for the fix next time and the time after that. In effect, if I provide the solutions, I *deprive* him of the chance to do it on his own. I also pass on an unspoken message to him that *I don't think he's capable* of fixing it on his own. It's a vote of no confidence. Dr. Haim Ginott, psychologist and author of many parenting books, says that what a child needs isn't "a guilty explanation or an instant solution...[He needs] the opportunity to exercise his autonomy, his own initiative. He need[s] to solve his own problem." He goes on to give parents shocking advice: "it's the parent's willingness to stand by silently while the child himself works out his own solution that is the greatest help."[1] Stand by silently? How do I do that when my child is distressed in any way whatsoever? This is the challenge of this step. Being still when every instinct I have says "take action" seems impossible! I go through all the options in my mind. What should I do? Should I intervene? I put this and every situation to a simple two-part test:

1. Is this a life-threatening situation? Is my child running out into traffic? Will he lose an eye, break a leg, or in some other way harm his own body? Will he harm someone else? Will he cause irreversible damage to his own or another's personal property? No. On all counts, this is not a dangerous situation from which he or someone else requires protection.

2. Is this something that he is capable of solving? Does he have the ability to handle this physically? Yes. Is he capable of navigating this emotionally? Yes. Will it be difficult for him, embarrassing and frustrating? Probably. It might even be humiliating and emotionally painful, but that's OK. If he is old enough to be able, and emotionally mature enough to know how, then I need to step out of his way. I must try to stand by silently and see what happens. I'm still not sure I can do this. God can. I guess I'll have to let Him.

Notice that Dr. Ginott doesn't say: do nothing, offer no support, let him deal with it himself. He says to stand by, which implies that I'm right there, at Will's side. I offer to listen. I gently acknowledge his evident upset. If he wants to vent or ask questions, I'm there. But I am a *silent* support. I do not impose my parental agenda, packed with worries, fantasies, fears and wishes, onto him at this point. I respect his need to talk or not talk. I offer, but don't insist.

Instead of going into fix-it mode, I waited. I did not mention it when Will came out of his room 20 minutes later, composed, to do his homework and have a snack. I did not mention it at dinner, nor afterward while he had his T.V. and playtime. At bedtime, I prayed for him as I always do, and I asked God to "help Will with whatever difficulty he had at school today. Give him wisdom and strength to sort it out and make it better." He did not comment, so again I was silent. Will went to sleep peacefully.

I had a more difficult time falling asleep, realizing (again) and struggling with how powerless I am over my child's life, especially the life that he lives when he is away from me. The only thing I have control over is me, my reactions, my feelings.

I repeated this mantra the next day, when I dropped Will off at school and tried to read Mrs. Adams' expression. It was patient and kindly, as always. Again, I struggled with the management of Will's life. I wanted to approach Mrs. Adams and ask her about the incident yesterday. I wanted to get into the middle of their relationship (hers and Will's) and make it *right*. Is this any of my business, how my child interacts with his teacher? Perhaps it is, if she invites me—or if he does. If she had sent a note home, asking for my intervention, it would have been different, but she had not. This was between them. I had to surrender it.

How difficult this surrender is! It's not so very different from an alcoholic surrendering his desire and "urge" to drink, or from a co-dependent's desire to control the person in her life who is drinking. Everything in our minds tells us that we should be able to fix things for our children, make them right, help them navigate through life. I don't want to surrender the relationship between Will and Mrs. Adams. What if he's really in trouble? What if he gets labeled as a problem student? What if he ends up on the clock tower, aiming a machine gun at Mrs. Adams (did you see the movie *Parenthood*? You really should) and ruining his life? What if, what if, what if…it's my favorite self-destructive mantra. I say self-destructive, because anything that takes me away from God and leading the life that I believe He wants me to lead will result in destroying that life.

So—surrender! Smile and nod at Mrs. Adams. Give Will a shoulder pat good-bye. Go to my car. Say a prayer: "I surrender, I let go." Go running at the park, repeating, "I surrender, I let go," about a hundred and seventy-six times. It's hard to surrender when I'm certain that it means I'm shirking my responsibility. Somehow, I believe that I'm responsible for my son's life. Every single bit of it. Even a 30-second conversation between him and his third grade teacher. What kind of ego does it take to believe that I'm responsible for *that*?

I know that you're dying to know the answers, the solutions for Jilly's parents and for Will's mom. I can't tell you exactly what happened for Will; I wasn't there. But I do know that he came home from school that day in a much different state of mind. In the car, he was chatty and engaging. I casually mentioned, "sounds like you had a good day with Mrs. Adams." He said, "yes," and kept on chatting about the current science experiment in growing cocoons. After a bit, he volunteered, "I just made up with Mrs. Adams, and then I tried to help her out a lot." Wow! He made up with her. He knows about making amends. How did he learn that? Maybe he has his own solutions that have nothing to do with me. Hmm.

With Jilly, the solution is unclear. Her parents are trying the institutional method. They've placed her in long-term care. I hope that it helps her. They are hoping, I believe, that the "experts" can control and manage their daughter. It's not an approach that will likely lead to Jilly taking control of her own problems, but it may be their best option at this point in their daughter's life. When a child's life is in jeopardy, the stakes change. The principle, however, does not.

~ I am powerless over my child,

and his or her life is unmanageable by me. ~

Chapter 2

"Insanity is repeating the same actions and expecting different results."

~ Benjamin Franklin

The second step:

I am willing to believe that a power greater than myself can restore me to sanity.

I am willing to believe that a power greater than myself...

For first-time 12-steppers (as well as for many who are veteran steppers), the concept of a power greater than ourselves is difficult to grasp. Some were agnostics or atheists. The fact of, or belief in, the existence of such a Power was doubtful, confusing, and even abhorrent to some. *Alcoholics Anonymous*, which is the basic tome and ideological foundation of all 12-step modeled programs, deals extensively with the "God concept" in a chapter devoted entirely to "We Agnostics." They talk of the necessity of finding a "spiritual basis of life"[1] in order to recover from alcoholism.

Although being a parent will hopefully not yield the same inevitably fatal consequences that practicing alcoholics face, and despite the fact that raising children is not usually a life-threatening condition, there are parallels to be found in the emotional and spiritual lives of many parents. I see parallels in the desperation, anxiety, and fears that parents bring to me when I teach workshops. I hear them wanting to know the "right way" to discipline, the "best way" to increase their child's self-esteem: they want the road map for producing a perfectly happy, productive, kind, respectful, successful child. They want this so much that they cannot parent because of conflicting information. Some teachers say to set boundaries, some say not to. Some spiritual leaders say to punish with a "rod," some say never to raise your voice. Some books say to send your kids off to daycare, others warn of dire problems that arise when you don't raise your child yourself. It's a terrifying, overwhelming state of parenting terror! Perhaps you have experienced some of this.

Alcoholics and addicts are said to reach a "bottom" before they finally "concede to their innermost selves"[1] that they are in need of help. This bottom is described as a spiritual, emotional, mental, and/or physical collapse that is so severe and painful that a person might not be able to recover from it without help. In my own experience, I reached my "parenting bottom" with my first son's developmental demonstration of his own willpower. *Alcoholics Anonymous* states that "lack of power…was our dilemma."[2] I felt this lack of power when Will was in the back seat, screaming and writhing and kicking, which I will detail in the next section. This lack of power and the resulting fearfulness, anxiety, and anger that I felt were the beginning of some extremely dispiriting emotions for me.

After I reacted (badly) to his temper tantrums, and spent several months trying to control either him and his outbursts or me and my reactions, I finally got to the point of *surrender* which was, for me, the only way I could truly be willing to ask my Higher Power to help me with this parenting thing. I cried, sobbed, felt sorry for myself, and wallowed in remorse (more on this later), but still I found it true, as the Big Book says: "we could will these things with all our might, but the needed power wasn't there. Our human resources, as marshaled by the will, were not sufficient; they failed utterly…We had to find a power by which we could live, and it had to be a power *greater than ourselves*."[3] I had found this power before, in a surrender in another 12-step program. I found that I had to ask Him to help me be a parent, because, clearly, I needed to be restored.

…can restore me to sanity.

For some of us, the insanity begins the moment the nurse places that yowling, red-faced, sticky little stranger into our arms. Who is this person? Why exactly is she crying? How can I stop it? Where did this overwhelming, heartache-y feeling of protectiveness come from?

For me, the insanity started even earlier. There were months of infertility treatment, urine testing, temperature taking, and feelings of despair at the arrival of a baby shower invitation or a passing stroller on the sidewalk. I remember that panicky feeling with each passing month that brought me closer to my 38th birthday. It'll never happen for me. I won't get to have a family. I've really messed up, and I'm not ever going to be fertile. This panic began the insanity for me. Every menstrual cycle, I would crumble into fits of sobs and melancholy. I stopped living my life. All I could focus on was the missing part of me—my motherhood. I stopped going to the baby showers. I never cooed over newborns. I started saying things like "oh, I'm not a baby person," or "I have dogs, I don't need kids."

When the infertility drug "worked," I was elated. At only five weeks pregnant, I told the world. We took the test! We're preggers! I jumped right into the fantasy of babyhood and mommyhood. Maternity clothes, baby stuff, furniture— shopping! At 12 weeks, I miscarried, and my world dissolved. I was a big sobbing mess of guilt and fear and anguish. My friend Beth held me while I cried and bled. My OB-GYN told me it was a temporary setback, that 1 out of 5 pregnancies miscarry, sometimes without the woman's knowledge that she was pregnant. It was cold comfort. I was certain this was a sign that I would **never** have children. Ever.

Even though I was sure I was doomed, I did begin to take my temperature again, test my urine, and have scheduled, regimented sex with my husband. I lost myself in the obsession of the baby. I did not enjoy the sex; all I could think of was my determination to make the sperm swim at the right angle at the right time (control over sperm? hmm). I was compulsively careful to keep my pelvis elevated for at least a half an hour afterward, and to keep myself from jumping, running, or in any way endangering the precious nesting going on inside me. It didn't work. I was an unhappy, angry woman. Although I hope my ever-patient husband enjoyed the procreation-oriented sex we kept having, I'm pretty sure he didn't enjoy the moody, single-minded woman I had become. I stopped enjoying most of my life. A few days before my period came each month, I would begin to be cautiously, hopefully optimistic. I allowed myself to "feel" pregnant. I relaxed and enjoyed my marriage and my life. But when my menses began, I would dip back down into the pit of infertile misery. Several months went by like this, and then a whole year. Things were very dark for me. I saw no purpose in my life if I couldn't be a mother. I wanted to die.

Several weeks later, my mother died. She had suffered several years of chemo treatments and radiation, but finally, the cancer won. We all cried. She was a kind and loving woman, a good, strong and sensible mom, and a dear, sweet human. I will never stop missing her. A daughter part of me died, too. I realized with such a depth of sorrow that my mom would never hold or cuddle or sing to my baby. I also realized that I had been in mourning for the last 18 months, and it was time to get back to life.

Finally, finally, I gave up! I asked God to restore me to sanity. I confessed my self-centered obsession with baby-making. I wrote about my sadness and emptiness. I admitted that I had been trying to control and manipulate nature and my ovaries. I saw that I had been arrogantly telling God that I knew what I needed. Now, instead, I asked God to fill me up with what He knew I needed. I told my husband I was sorry I had created such a one-sided relationship. We began to talk about adoption. It was something I had never been willing to look at. We met a lovely adoption counselor, and discussed all our options. That night, we went home and really talked about what our life might look like in ways that I had never allowed.

Sometime after that night, I conceived. As you might imagine, the 38 weeks that followed were filled with joy, morning sickness, lots of shopping, and plenty of anxiety. Constantly, in the back of my mind, I carried the fear of the first miscarriage. Constantly, I worried that I wouldn't be a good enough mother. The insanity kept nipping at my heels.

Some describe insanity as the process of "repeating the same actions and expecting different results," or failure to learn from your mistakes. If you go to a well to get a bucket of water and the well is dry, will you go again to the same well? Maybe once. Maybe even twice. But hopefully, at some point, you'll look for a different source. You'll say to yourself, "Hmmm. I don't want to spend fifteen minutes walking over to that well when I know there won't be any water. I'll try going to the Sparkletts water cooler jar instead." But in the everyday variety of insanity, we return again and again to methods, procedures, and even fantasies or dreams that don't work. We keep trying to control the uncontrollable.

Fast-forward through a few years. Will was born healthy, undamaged by my worry (another worry), and with wide, grey eyes looking around the delivery room. He had colic, learned to sleep through the night, began walking and talking on schedule, and then his brother Jamie was born. Will was almost three. The first year of Jamie's life was a blur. I was a sleep-deprived, wrinkled, fat, milky blob. Will was turning into an inquisitive, loquacious, engaging preschooler. He talked to everyone he met, told them his opinions, and asked millions of questions. For awhile, I thought I could handle two children. That was before Will started telling me why he was going to be in charge of his own self.

This declaration came with his first bona fide temper tantrum. He was in the back seat. Jamie was at home with a sitter. We were on our way back from Mommy & Me time, and I needed to get home quickly because I could feel the milk building up. Will had not wanted to leave the Mommy & Me class, and now he didn't want to go home. He expressed this feeling to me in a clear and visceral way. He started screaming and kicking his heels in the car seat. His body writhed, and his back arched. He was saying something like "GO BACK—Go Back—Go Back—Gooo Baaaaack!!" I was trying to drive up the hill. There were cars behind me. I felt like I was going to explode. I stopped the car and began screaming back at him, saying stupid, idiotic things, like: "We can't go back. We have to go home. I have to feed Jamie. You have to stop screaming. Do you want a time out? Do you want to give up your T.V. time? Will, STOP IT!" He could hear none of these things. He was a screaming, kicking, writhing mass of ANGRY! He couldn't hear my adult explanations and threats, yet I kept trying to explain it to him over and over. Finally, I lost my temper, grabbed his little legs, smacked his bottom, and yelled in his face. He stopped tantrumming and just began to sob. It was a forlorn, surrendered cry. I got back into the front seat, shaking badly, and finished driving home. Will napped when we got home. I fed Jamie. I felt so remorseful. I had vowed never to strike my children, and I had given in to my own rage and desperation. I tried to make it up to Will by being extra patient with him, but it was really not needed. He had forgotten about the tantrum, and went about his busy 3-year-old day. His equilibrium was reestablished. I re-vowed never to lose my temper or hit my children.

This is the insanity part. The tantrum scenario played

out over and over for the next several months. Each time, I would try "reasoning" with Will. Then, I would threaten him with time outs, or missing a birthday party, or some such meaningless threat. Then, I would lose my temper too, and yell or shout or slam the door, or drag him physically from the mall or grocery store. I didn't hit him again, but nonetheless, I felt frustrated, sad, remorseful, and so alone. I was out of self-control. I felt like the worst mother in the world.

Sophocles, a Greek philosopher of the fifth century B.C., said that "children are the anchors that hold a mother to life."[4] This statement holds much wisdom and understanding of the bond between most mothers and children, but it can also describe the torture of that relationship. After all, an anchor can pull you down into the depths, can it not? Being a new mother who had tried so hard to become one, I desperately wanted to do the right thing, provide the right discipline, be the kind of mother I remembered (and idealized) my own mother was. Many days, I felt as if I were drowning from the anchors I had borne. I had nowhere to turn. I had once again said and done things that I didn't want to do. I had heard and felt my rage come out of me like an uncontainable dragon. I had pulled my toddler by his arms out of the car because he refused to get out, or roared at him until the baby in my arms cried in fear, or bullied him into his room and, on the way, he had screamed "I hate you!" These were the times when I truly wondered if I was going insane. I wasn't sure what a nervous breakdown felt like, but I was pretty certain I was close. Some days, as the boys played outside, I would look forlornly over the gate at our driveway, wishing for *anyone* to walk by so I could say "hi" and invite them in. I was *lonely*; I spent so many hours being a mom that I wasn't sure I was me anymore. I had turned into this confusing, amorphous combo plate of sentimental love, adoration, despair, and rage. In the darkest of these moments, I wondered if my children would be better off without me.

I began to wonder if God had made a mistake in letting me have children. Maybe I had "tricked" Him into thinking I could handle it. Perhaps, I reasoned, He knew better, and that's why it had been so difficult for me to conceive. Maybe He just became weary of my relentless petitions, and He (as any exhausted parent is tempted to do) finally caved in.

Or maybe He was allowing me my pain and anguish so that I could be surrendered enough to learn something.

Years later, while teaching parenting classes, I met John and Mary Lou. They, too, had waited a long time to have children. When they finally conceived, they were joyous. Her pregnancy, childbirth, and early years with Taylor were uneventful. They loved being parents. Taylor, they told me, was a loving and "easy" child. She had learned to walk early. She was talking in full sentences by 20 months, and she was physically very agile. She was now a little bit over two, and they were starting to have difficulties because she would not "listen," so they came to parenting class to learn how to make her become more compliant. One evening, they had a question about how to teach Taylor to stay in the house. I was curious, and inquired what they meant.

"Well," said John, "now that it's warmer in the evenings, we leave the front door open. The screen is closed, but the latch doesn't lock the door."

"So last week," continued Mary Lou, "Taylor figured out how to open the screen door and let herself outside."

"We told her 'no' and diverted her back into the house several times."

"Did that help?" I asked.

"No!" John exclaimed. As soon as we would go back into the dining room or somewhere else, she would go back to the door and open it again. She's done it a dozen times this week!"

"It was awful, because one time we weren't paying attention, and she got halfway down the block before we went after her!" The parenting group emitted an audible gasp.

"What should we do to teach her not to go out the door?" asked John.

"We tried a time out. That didn't work. We even tried slapping her hand," sighed an exasperated Mary Lou. "Why can't she be obedient?"

What does this sound like? Repeating the same actions and expecting different results. It's a parent's version of insanity. My suggestion of how to curtail this curious two-year-old's behavior? Install a lock on the screen door so she can't open it up.

A two-year-old is not developmentally ready to understand that her actions are causing the consequences. She may be able to stop her behavior in the moment that her mother slaps her hand or yells at her to "stop," but she cannot mentally store that information and act on it tomorrow when she sees a hummingbird at the feeder outside, and she wants to open the door by herself to go and get it. Like most children, two-year-olds live "in the moment." They do not think, "yesterday, my mommy got mad because I went out the door." They think, simply, "look—pretty birdie—I'm going to go and get it." It was not an act of disobedience that Taylor continued opening the door, but an act of curiosity.

Similarly, my three-year-old tantrumming in the back of my car, screaming at the mall, or stomping his little feet in my kitchen could not stop himself. My repeated actions to try and get him to stop were an exercise in futility. They didn't control his tantrums, they didn't help me control my own reaction, and they always left me feeling regret and sadness. The well was dry, and it was time to go somewhere else. It was time to put a lock on the screen door, admit that I was powerless over my three-year-old and his life was unmanageable by me, and become willing to be humble enough to know that only a Power greater than myself could restore me (and him) to sanity.

Sometimes, a parent can come to this realization quickly, and with an abrupt "ah-ha," can change directions. Not I. For me, coming to admit that I'm powerless and then seeing that I'm actually over the edge and vaulting toward insanity is excruciatingly difficult. I arrive at this admission only through pain. It has gotten easier, though, since I've been working on these steps. Sometimes, I can even see the pain coming, and begin working like crazy to surrender. Sometimes. Other times, I have to go the traditional route with a lot of tears, feelings of remorse and regret, and then prayers, journal-writing, and more prayers until I can finally believe and even accept the trusty, time-honored credo: "I surrender, I let go."

Chapter 3

"The constant effort to get a child to do what I consider vital and he considers superfluous can knock the cheer out of you."

~ *Adele Faber/Elaine Mazlish*

The third step:

I am decided to turn my child's life and will over to the care of God, *as I understand Him.*

What an order! Turning my child's life and will over to the care of *anyone* besides me takes a huge leap of faith. It's one of those precepts that I must practice daily, because daily, I pull that decision back to me and decide that I *should* be in control. I *can* master their lives. I *am* the only one who knows how to do it. After all, I bore their bodies inside me for 40 weeks, I delivered them into the world, I fed them from my own breasts, I, I, I. It's all about me, right? Yes, it's my ego that's on the line, here. As I always remind my husband, the public endorsement of that motherly "guidance" (a.k.a.: power and control) is when the football jock lovingly says to the camera: "Hi, Mom!" and we all say: "Awwww."

Let's start with that original, arrogant assumption: I bore their bodies. Yes. And who created me to be a mother? Who decided how and when and to whom I would be a mother? If I go back to the origin of time, I will never be able to answer that question. But I do remember those desperate infertile days, and think that I was finally able to conceive when I let go of the notion of my own control. Damn! There's that issue again.

The "cheerless coexistence" that Faber and Mazlish so eloquently describe in their books is the mood that penetrates my home when I'm determined to "make him" do it *my* way: when it's My Will be Done, not Thy Will. Power and control are the culprits. As we discussed in Step 1, they are really illusions; I can control only those things that *I* do, prepare, say, advocate, etc. Let's look at the world-famous "Serenity Prayer:"[1]

> God,
>
> Grant me the serenity to accept
> The things I cannot change,
> The courage to change
> The things I can,
> And the wisdom
> To know the difference.

Accept the things I cannot change

This prayer, written anonymously almost a century ago, contains all the wisdom needed to accomplish the third step. First, you have to accept what you cannot change. This is simple; you cannot change "other people, places and things," as the 12-step response goes. In the case of my children, I must accept who they are. I cannot change their basic disposition or character, their feelings, or their view of the world. I cannot change their attitudes when they wake up "in a mood." I have a limited ability to impact their lives. I must accept their choices in friendship, fashion, playthings, study interests, and later, their affections, loves, lifestyles, and career choices. If I am in tune with who my child is, I will learn from her how to be her mother.

We had a boy in our carpool in elementary school.

He was a nice little boy, and I liked his mother very much. She was always positive, active in sports, and outgoing. Her boy, Todd, was not. His usual response to me in the morning was silence or a grumpy "hi," and when asked how his weekend was, or his morning, or almost anything, Todd invariably replied "bad." At first, this shocked and bothered me, and I tried to talk him out of his bad mood. "Surely there must be something good that happened this weekend?" "Not really," he'd dolefully reply. If I pressed him, he'd become silent. Todd was on Will's soccer team in third grade, and I remember occasionally driving them to games together. Todd was usually complaining about how much he hated soccer, and how he wished he could just stay at home.

Todd's natural disposition was neither cheerful nor athletic. Todd's mother was not in acceptance about this. She was convinced that eventually he would come to love sports as much as she did. Her daughter, Joey, was much more like her in temperament. Joey loved baseball, soccer, basketball. She loved to run around and jump and play. She immediately took to sports and excelled at them. Joey and her mom were naturally alike.

They were similar in many of the same aspects in which Todd and his mother were naturally unalike. Bruno Bettleheim, noted child psychologist, discusses this dissonance:

> Even if a parent insists that his view of a given issue is to prevail and his rules are to be obeyed, this does not guarantee that the child accepts any of this in his heart. As far as inner experience is concerned, child and parent each follow their own rules, usually without these rules having been made explicit either to themselves or to the other. [2]

These conflicts or variances in the "rules" may have created an internal tension for Todd that he could not resolve. He had a desire, I'm sure, to please his mother, but this was lost to the conflicts that arose between them. It's possible that these conflicts started in infancy. D.W. Winnicott, pediatrician and developmental theorist, authored many books on the way infant-mother bonds are formed. He says that a baby's "good start" in life "is assured in nature by the existence of the bond between the baby's mother and the baby." [3] These two psychologists and many others talk about the importance of this bond, and how it affects the way a child views himself as he develops. It may be that Todd's mother did not have the capacity for bonding with Todd in the way that he needed. The "fit" between baby and mother may not have been adequate for him.

Unable to please his mother because of this uneven pairing, he became depressed, resentful and then defiant. When he started into middle school at 12, he began acting out with drugs and alcohol, and getting into trouble at school with a "bad crowd" of kids. Todd's mother asked me not long ago what I thought had caused Todd's recent bad behavior. Was it her fault? Was she a bad mother? She said she had done every thing she knew how to do. She had taken her kids to temple, had disciplined them when they misbehaved and had tried to keep them active in sports and other activities so "they wouldn't have time to get into trouble." She had lectured and scolded, praised and rewarded. She had tried to be a good mother.

I assured her that it wasn't her fault. I told her that Todd's path was his own, and she had not caused him to turn to drugs any more than she had caused her daughter Joey to enjoy basketball so much that she was about to be in tournament play-offs for their region. Each child had different temperaments and interests. Each had his or her own personality. And each child had his or her own path.

> Winnicott's model of the "good enough mother...starts off with an almost complete adaptation to her infant's needs, and as time

proceeds, she adapts less and less completely, gradually, according to the infant's growing ability to deal with her failure." [4]

Given that their temperaments were so different, it may have been virtually impossible for Todd's mother to be attuned to his needs when he was a baby. When he had colic as an infant, for instance, she may have given up on trying to soothe him, and left him alone in his crib to "cry it out." When he wasn't ready to toilet train, it's possible that she was overly harsh in her criticism of him. These are only some possible examples of mis-attunement; I didn't witness Todd's infancy and early childhood.

I do know, though, that when Todd was negative or grumpy, his mom criticized him in front of the other boys he played with. I heard her say upon occasion, "what does he have to be complain about? He has no reason to be so unhappy," when he tried to express to her that he didn't want to do something. I witnessed times when she "forced him" to participate in sports and school activities in which he was disinterested. I saw him become frustrated with these activities to the point of anger and resentment. In short, Todd's mom did not accept his interests, abilities, or his temperament. She was convinced (unconsciously, I'm fairly certain) that she could control these things.

To the extent that we try to control and manipulate someone else's behavior, we cease to allow him his *self*. We are telling him, in essence, that who he is, is not good enough. This is the message that Todd's mother sent him in many ways throughout his childhood: You are not who I want you to be. Be different. What choice did Todd have when he reached adolescence? He could have given over his spirit and tried against his own self to become who his mother needed, or he could rebel and feel the freedom of being himself. He chose the favored route of teen rebellion.

Is it possible that Todd would have turned to drugs,

alcohol and bad company even if his mom had been better attuned to who he was? Of course. It's possible that Todd's naturally (possibly chemically) lethargic and depressive personality would have been drawn to the same self-destructive outlets as a teenager. But might he have chosen a different path if his mother had intentionally tried to understand and parent his *self*? Acceptance could have been the key for them both.

The courage to change the things I can

Yea! I can now find some things that I can actually control! No, sorry to disappoint you, but the control is still an illusion—except, that is, for self-control. This is the portion of the prayer where you can take the reins and assert some of your self-power.

Things I can change: what to have for dinner, whether I pick up my kids from school on time, how I react when my (imaginary) daughter tells me that her friend Samantha hurt her feelings and she's going to tell Ellie that Sam is a snot, what I will say when Jamie pulls a pillow over his head and says "just smother me because my life is over," whether I will lie to the ticket person at Disneyland and tell him that I have a child under 12. I can affect all these things and more. I can influence my children with my behavior, attitudes, and respect for them. I have the courage to respond in an adult, appropriate way, most of the time. I don't have to be perfect at this. I know no one can. But I do have to try. I have to "work my steps," as 12-steppers say, to the best of my ability so that I can be proud of who I am as a mom.

- **modeling as a tool for change**

If I curse freely, it is only right that my children learn this from me. If I respect my husband and show him love and affection when he is home, they will learn this too. In essence, *modeling*, or acting out the behavior that I would like to see my kids embrace, is the best parenting tool I have.

Teaching my child to be polite is an excellent

example of how modeling can work. Dr. Ginott says a parent "cannot teach politeness rudely." If Aunt Joan has taken your son to the movies, for example, it is rude and ineffective to direct your child to "say thank you to Aunt Joan, Sammy." This form of 'negative' modeling teaches your child that it's ok to humiliate others for forgetting their manners. It's ok for an adult to embarrass a child.

More positive modeling would be to give the thanks to Aunt Joan yourself, in front of Sammy. He may automatically thank her as well. If not, you can remind him privately (at a later time) that you expect him to remember to thank people for favors he receives.[5]

The other lesson here is respect for a child's immediate state of mind. Once, when leaving a friend's house with Jamie, I stood in the driveway, thanking her for feeding Jamie lunch, arranging for another time to play, and hoping that Jamie would in turn thank her for the fun time. He and his friend, Harrison had enjoyed several hours of play. He did not offer any thanks. He had a Batman action figure, and was "zooming" Batman through the skies and across our car's window ledge as we got into the car. I kept making spaces for Jamie to say his thank you's, but the time to leave could not be postponed. Finally, I pulled out of the driveway, frustrated that my attempted modeling had yielded no perfunctory politeness from James. I mentioned as much to him. He responded, simply, "Mom, Batman doesn't say 'thank you.'" In his time frame and imagination, Jamie had no room for mere human manners. If I can accept his lapse in judgment, this too models something for my boy: acceptance.

- **listening as a tool for change**

In order to establish *therapeutic rapport* with their clients, a therapist will spend many sessions in an active form of listening. This requires observation of a client's mannerisms, body language, and facial expressions, as well as her choice of words, colloquialisms, emphasis on phrases, etc. A therapist is trained to listen to all of the client's linguistic cues, even the ones that aren't verbal. Think for example of a simple sentence: "I don't like that." Say it to yourself with the emphasis on different parts of the sentence: "*I* don't like that." I don't like *that*." Imagine crossing your arms as you say it. Or shaking your head. Or even, as a child might, stamping your foot as you scream it out loud. Then think of saying, simply, with no intonation: "I don't like that." What a difference it makes to hear this sentence (or any other) with all of your listening ability.

Your ability to listen to your child with all of your senses tuned is a tool that can promote great change—both for your child and for you as a parent. Look at this exchange between Will (age 3) and me in a department store checkout line:

"Mommy, what's that for?" He was looking at a large yellow pipe, which was attached at the corner of the store next to our cash register.

"I don't know, honey."

"Is it a water pipe? Do you think it's for water?"

"I'm not sure."

"Would the firemen use that if there was a fire? I saw a fire plug thing like that on Sesame Street. They hooked it up to a hose. All of this water came out fast. It was so fast that Big Bird was flying up in the air on the end of the hose. It was funny, Mommy. Did you see it?"

"Hmmm." (I'm distracted, trying to let the clerk know that I'm next in line, and he should take my stuff from my hands.)

"If there's a fire in the store, how could the trucks come in? Where would they fit? I don't think they could get in the store. Do you think their hoses are long enough to get all the way in here from their trucks?"

"I don't know."

"Mommy! How would we get out? Where do all of the people go? Do they all leave in the escalator? How do the firemen get in? And where will they plug in their hoses?"

By this time, I could've easily screamed: at Will, the salesclerk, the lady in line next to me—at the world! In fact, the salesclerk at this point rolled his eyes at me, motioned to Will and said: "Does he *always* ask this many questions?" It was a perfect opening for me to vent ("YES! And he's driving me nuts!") or to roll my eyes in irritation, but I just smiled, looked down at Will's little inquisitive face, and said: "Yes—he's really interested in all sorts of things, aren't you?" This modeled patience, interest in his curiosity, and tolerance. Listening is a small skill, but one with great impact.

The wisdom to know the difference

The question for the final part of the Serenity Prayer is: can I discern the things that I have control over (me) from the things that I do not (my child's temperament, character, and individual *self*)? This is the "wisdom to know the difference," which is the goal of step 3. This wisdom is not always easily learned, I discovered in my own parenting life. The hardest part about getting to this wisdom is acquiring the humility to realize that God is the father and the mother. I am merely His human representative on earth and caretaker of His child. I cannot do this on my own.

The AA "Third Step Prayer" [6] has been very helpful to me at times when I cannot find His way:

God, I offer myself to thee,
To build with me and to do with me as Thou wilt.
Relieve me of the bondage of self,
That I may better do Thy will.
Take away my difficulties that victory over them
May bear witness to those I would help
Of Thy Power, Thy Love and Thy Way of life.
May I do thy will always!

This prayer is the *decision to surrender* that I talked about in Step 2. It contains the admission that we are powerless, bound up in our own self-will, and that we need God to show us how to be, so that we can be witnesses of His power, love, and way of life. It asks for help from Him, because we are weak and so often stray from what He wants from us. Our weakness is the "bondage of self," which includes our most profound character flaws, or "defects" as the book *Alcoholics Anonymous* tells us. We are fearful, we are greedy. We worry, we obsess. Our fears invariably revolve around what will be taken away from us, or what we will never be able to acquire or achieve. Our children suffer the consequences of these fears and our resulting flawed behavior:

Mark insists that his son achieve at least a 4.0 grade point average and join the National Honor Society because he's afraid that he won't get into a good college where he can mix with the "right kind of people."

Anna won't allow her son to buy a car for his own use, even though he has earned the money himself and can afford the insurance. (She's afraid that he'll become too independent and not be around the family any more.)

Josh wants his wife to "control" her daughter's clingy-ness and leave her with a new sitter, even though she cries disconsolately. (He's fearful that his wife is transferring all of her affection to their daughter.)

Nicole tells her 10-year-old son that he should sleep with her when he's at her house because he'll be less afraid. (She hasn't felt safe since her divorce.)

These are some of the forms of "bondage of self" that this prayer is talking about. We will deal with them in depth in the next several steps.

Many times, in parental frustration and powerlessness, I have turned to this step. I can almost feel the peace fall on me as I surrender my child to Him who made both me and my son. Just to remember that my earthly, undisciplined, messy, disrespectful, unruly, disobedient son is a divine child of the Ruler of the Universe gives me hope. This surrender is simple (although not easy) when I insert the names of my children into the 3rd step prayer:

> God, I offer (my children) to Thee,
> To build with them and to do with them as Thou wilt.
> Relieve (child's name) of the bondage of self,
> That he/she may better do Thy will.
> Take away his/her difficulties that victory over them
> May bear witness to those he/she would help
> Of Thy Power, Thy Love and Thy Way of life.
> May (child's name) do thy will always!

Many times, I have made this surrender on my knees, with tears of mommy frustration and exasperation, and even resentment dribbling down my nose. Many times, I have asked God to do for me what I cannot do for myself: to see my child as His, relinquish my human desire for control, and ask for His help in summoning courage, strength, and patience to see this parenting job through.

Part II — Clean House

"Our growth in self-knowledge must inevitably result in a better comprehension of our children, even more so when the new insights are in consequence of experiences involving these children."

~ *Bruno Bettleheim*

Chapter 4

"We can accept that our children will have much less control than we do, as long as their behavior does not awaken in us feelings we wish to keep repressed; but when our own repressions become remobilized, we can no longer deal realistically with the negativism of our children."

~ *Bruno Bettleheim*

The fourth step

I'm willing to make a searching and fearless moral inventory of myself.

This step, and the next few steps that follow (specifically 4 through 9), are traditionally called the housecleaning steps; they require that you look at your own childhood, background, and accumulated issues to find your flaws, resentments, and the sources of your frustrations. The "searching and fearless moral inventory" that this step begins and the others continue is mandatory in the program of Alcoholics Anonymous for overcoming the disease of alcoholism and the "wreckage" that this disease has produced in the lives of the alcoholic and all those who care about him or her. [1]

Similarly, as a parent, I want to avoid passing along my own generational inheritance of anger, frustration, impatience and other character flaws. Renowned author Alice Miller says this inheritance results from "poisonous pedagogy" of authoritarian parenting. But, she says, if:

> ...as survivors of severe childhood humiliations we all too readily make light of, don't kill ourselves or others, are not drug addicts or criminals...we can still function as **dangerous carriers of infections**. We will continue to infect the next generation with the virus of "poisonous pedagogy" as long as we claim that this kind of upbringing is harmless. It is here that we experience the harmful aftereffects of our survival, because we can protect ourselves from a poison only if it clearly labeled as such, not if it is mixed, as it were, with ice cream and advertised as being "for Your Own Good." [2]

If I don't want to continue to carry this infection, the first thing I have to do is admit that I'm infected. This is difficult, because it means breaking down the denial, or repression, as Miller terms it, that I carry with me always. This denial takes many forms. In some cases, a childhood is completely forgotten, except perhaps for a few flashes of memory. We simply place all anxiety, anger, and fear into our unconscious memory, where they will sleep away the years. A woman I knew from a family process group had virtually no memories of childhood. Although severely depressed in new sobriety, she was at a loss to explain why. She knew that she had many scars, both emotional and physical, and she was aware that she'd had many "accidents" as a child. As she became more physically sober, her memory gradually returned in photo-like bits. They were not happy memories: she had been brutally abused by both parents. The process of unearthing and facing those memories was horrifying to her, and it was very difficult to remain committed to her sober life. With many nurturing caretakers around her, and dedication to 12-step work, she is now a healthy, productive adult.

In other cases, repression is more subtle. Peter, a man born in the years right after the Great Depression, often refers to his parents as "self-sacrificing," having traded away their worldly goods to keep food on the table for their children. Peter describes his parents as "strict and stern," but defends them as doing what "parents should do, because you can't 'spare the rod' or your kids will be ruined." In turn, he too, sacrificed for his own children, working at a job that was dissatisfying for a boss who was demanding and ruthless. Now retired, widowed, and clinically depressed, Peter states: "I had a good childhood. I had good parents. I have no reason to be depressed." He has no compassion for his own pain. His anger, frustration, and disappointment are denied existence because they would be too painful to look at.

Our tendency as children is to protect and idealize our parents. We believe the underlying message that our parents' unrealistic expectations imply: we need to do better. When they are critical of our behavior, we assume we are to blame, that we are bad or naughty. If they are overbearing and demanding, we feel compelled to perform better in school, to play harder on the field, to win more, to score higher. If they are critical or harsh, we know that we are not good children. This is the how the twisty vine of denial grows. Our own badness, imperfections, and naughtiness are unacceptable. We need to set them aside, disown them, repress them so we can become perfect children who will make our parents happy with us, which will yield a "happy childhood and a normal family."

When asked by my therapist many years ago about my childhood, I instantly replied, "it was a normal, happy childhood," and in many instances it was. But to term it "happy" belies the distress I felt every time my father was drunk and out of control, or so angry that he injured one of my brothers. It gives no validation to my own turmoil, disappointment, anger and frustration that were never allowed expression in my home. Miller says that parents are "helpless when it comes to understanding their child so long as they must keep the sufferings of their own childhood at an emotional distance." ³

In order to give voice to these sufferings, the fourth step begins the process of housecleaning (or maybe we should more accurately term it "character cleaning") by suggesting that I write them down. This writing can be as formal or informal as you wish, but it is important that it be "searching and fearless."

It may help to write it as an "autobiography," starting with your earliest memory of a resentment, hurt feeling, or angry moment. Don't be frightened to look at every moment in your childhood that still holds some emotional impact in your memory. If it is something that you remember strongly, it is probably important to write down.

There are three kinds of emotional memories to write about thoroughly: resentments, fears, and hurts. The word "resentment" is derived from the root word "sentir," which means to feel; thus, to "resent" is to "re-feel" something. Usually the emotion that you are re-experiencing is negative, and is the result of an insult, hurt or offense to you. It's the retention of these feelings of bitterness or anger or hurts that we hold inside of ourselves until they are "triggered" by something your child does or says. We then react in a way that in turn injures them. Writing them is the first part of getting rid of them.

Allow me to use some examples from my own inventory. The first one that comes to my mind is when my mother slapped my thigh for talking back to her. As I remember it, I wanted to do something and she wouldn't allow me to, so I expressed my disappointment in a typical teenage manner: I rolled my eyes and used a snotty tone of voice to let her know how idiotic I thought her to be. Her response was a sharp slap on my thigh. My counter-response was scalding anger and resentment. I can still feel how much I hated her in that moment. The second and third incidents I've written down are self-explanatory.

In autobiographical style, my inventory of these items would be just like this:

I'm angry at:

Mom, *for slapping my thigh when I was 13 because I "talked back"*

Dad, *for scaring me when I was 7 or 8. He backed me into a closet and left me there*

My music teacher, *who ridiculed me in front of the class for holding the bow incorrectly*

If you prefer to use a less wordy method, write everything down in a chart format. The example below paraphrases the inventory in the book of *Alcoholics Anonymous*:

I'm angry at:	Incident:
Mother	She hit me when I "talked back" to her about her decision.
Dad	He scared me when he backed me into the closet. He left me there.
Teacher	Ridiculed me in front of class for holding violin bow incorrectly.

Begin with the "I'm angry at" column on the left. There will be three sections for your entire inventory, one for each of the three headings: "I'm angry at," "I'm resentful of," and "I'm hurt because." I started with the "anger" section. I think back to an early memory of someone with whom I was angry, and remember what the incident was that is still in my conscience. Then I list the people in this column who come to mind. As I write down the people, I also note the incident or event that engendered such strong emotions for me.

It's most important to list your parents or caretakers. This is where you inherited most of your attitudes and behaviors that affect your current parenting. However, if you've never done a thorough housecleaning before, it will be helpful to do so now. For example, you may still be angry at your third grade teacher for putting you in the corner for chewing gum, or with your best friend from fourth grade for borrowing a dollar and never paying you back. It doesn't matter how "silly" your intellectual self tells you it is; if you still "feel" it, it's important to write it.Next, add another column that lists the emotional response you had to each incident. For example:

I'm angry at:	Incident:	My response:
Mother	She hit me when I "talked back" to her about her decision.	angry, powerless, ashamed
Dad	He scared me when he backed me into the closet. He left me there.	insecure, upset, fearful
Teacher	Ridiculed me in front of class for holding violin bow incorrectly.	angry, humiliated, clumsy, stupid

Sometimes, the emotional response you had may be the same one as this section—i.e., anger. In this case, you may leave this column blank.

Add a fourth column that identifies how your character or sense of self was affected by the remembered incident. In some cases, I cannot remember what my feelings were, or what was affected. For any event, you can leave columns blank. You don't need to over-think this; just write what comes to your mind. The Big Book says that "God constantly discloses more to you and to us,"[4] and I've found this to be true. Something long-forgotten will be brought to my mind by an event, or a dream, or a sudden flash of memory. As it is said, when the "pupil is ready, the teacher appears."

I'm angry at:	Incident:	My response:	Affects my:
Mother	She hit me when I "talked back" to her	angry, powerless shame	not sure (?)
Dad	He scared me when he backed me into the closet	insecure, upset fearful	sense of security
Teacher	Ridiculed me in front of class . . .	angry, humiliated clumsy, stupid	self-esteem love of music

Finally, add a column that addresses your own responsibility in the incident. In many of these cases, I'm unaware of my "part;" I may have been too young to understand, or perhaps I have just forgotten. In these cases, I can list "unknown," or I can simply say that my part is "holding on" to the hurt, anger or resentment.

I'm angry at:	Incident:	My response:	Affects my:	My part:
Mother	She hit me when I "talked back" to her	angry, powerless shame	not sure	I was disrespectful
Dad he backed me into the closet	He scared me when fearful	insecure, upset	security "holding on"	?? Not sure
Teacher	Ridiculed me in front of class . . .	angry, humiliated clumsy, stupid	self-esteem love of music	I didn't practice; laziness

When "my part" is not obvious, it may be because my parent or another caretaker did something to me that had nothing to do with me. I am legitimately not responsible in any way. I might have been happily bouncing my tennis ball on the driveway, and Dad became frustrated because he wanted to park in the garage. I can't remember doing anything "wrong." I remember only his excessive reaction and my feelings.

There are two important considerations about adding the fifth column. "My Part" isn't intended to be used as a weapon to beat yourself over the head! Children are messy, lazy, self-centered, and ill-mannered. They do not have the perspective of an adult, nor have they developed the self-discipline that their parents (hopefully) will teach them. So, although my "laziness" (third entry, "my part") at not practicing the violin was an issue that may have initiated the scene with my teacher, she, as an adult, should have had the forbearance to correct me without humiliation or public ridicule.

The second consideration when writing out this fifth column is in the case of an abusive parent. When you are an abused child, "my part" is not pertinent. **There is no amount of good behavior that will affect the reactions of an abusive parent.** Hopefully, in writing out an inventory, you will recognize abuse if it existed. There is no benefit in identifying "your part" when facing the irrational rage of an abusive parent. It's important to list the offenses. Then, you can clearly see the behaviors and distinguish the words or actions that might be triggers for you as a parent. It's also important to list them so that you can begin to release them. If you recognize, perhaps for the first time, that you were an abuse victim, it may be helpful or even necessary to contact a mental health professional while working on this inventory. Powerful feelings and uncontainable behaviors may result from excavating the past. If you suspect this may be true for you, you had best find a therapist to guide and support you through this process.

You may feel, as I once did, that this exercise is an excessive self-indulgence in the emotions of the past. You may also feel, as many do, that psychotherapy is akin to self-pity, that wallowing around in past hurts and grudges is not productive for living a happy, positive life. I submit that if you are reading this book, it is precisely because you are not at that goal. There is something in your way. My guess is that you do not want that "something" to impede your child's happiness as well, so think of this inventory as a way to unload your past hurts, not to wallow in them.

The fact that you know there are hurts in your past, and you think that you have "come to terms" with them, doesn't necessarily mean that they are truly resolved. Many times, we reenact these hurts upon our children without meaning to. This is precisely because our "intellectual knowledge is no guarantee of understanding and tolerance." 5 There is also no guarantee of avoiding passing these things on. Let's look at Treva's childhood for a minute.

Treva grew up as a foster child. Her mother died when she was about 5. She "doesn't remember" what happened, but she has heard stories from other family members that her father killed her mother when he caught her with another man. He has been in prison for all of Treva's remembered life. She was raised primarily by an aunt and uncle. They moved Treva and her two brothers in with them, a few hours away from where she had lived until then. Treva's Aunt Sarah had three children of her own, and was a working mom who had very little tolerance for disorder, noise, and disobedience. Treva "tried to be good," but she was always being too messy or too loud; she was then "disciplined," which consisted of spankings and/or lectures, which made her feel stupid and humiliated. She generally felt out of place at school and at home. "It was a good childhood," she assured me in an early session. "My aunt and uncle didn't have to take me in. They fed me and sent me to Catholic school, just like their real kids. And yeah, they spanked me, but it was so I would grow up good and strong."

This phrase came to haunt me as Treva told me stories of growing up with very few personal possessions, dominance bordering on cruelty rendered by her older boy cousins, and frequent torment at a nearly all-white school in which she was one of a few mixed-race students. Her continual insistence that "they didn't have to take me in" echoed like a refrain that had probably been told to her dozens of times by a tired, resentful, over-stressed aunt who was angry about raising more children than she could afford. Treva's solution during middle school was to start "hanging out with the stoners," not so much to get high, but to have a place to belong. She soon found a boyfriend with whom she became pregnant, and at age 14, she gave birth to a son. Ill-equipped to care for a baby, she left the infant at her aunt's house and got on a bus to the closest large city. Here, she lived on the streets for five years before finding a shelter and beginning to try to turn her life around. Now, at age 20, she is pregnant again and is determined to "be a good mother" to this child. I find this resolve admirable, and I've told her so, but I think the possibility of it happening is limited. She has neither a positive role model for being a mother or the inclination to look at her own injuries and learn from them.

> The conviction that parents are always right, that every act of cruelty, whether conscious or unconscious, is an expression of their love, is deeply rooted in human beings because it is based on the process of internalization that takes place in the first months of life. [6]

Because of this conviction, it is very difficult for parents like Treva to commit to the introspection necessary to uncover the past. Because of the pain involved in doing so, their uncovering, and thus their recovery, is seldom completed.

Chapter 5

"When a woman had to suppress and repress all these needs in relation to her own mother, they rise from the depth of her unconscious and seek gratification through her own child, however well-educated and well-intentioned she may be, and however much aware she is of what a child needs."

~ Alice Miller

The fifth step

I admit to God, to myself, and to another human being the exact nature of my wrongs.

As step 4 was about housecleaning, this step is about dumping the trash! Now that you have made a list of all those childhood injuries, feelings, hurts, and misdeeds, it's time to expel them from the place they have taken in your life. This may seem like an enormous task, but it is very necessary. Think of the contents of all those trash bags after you have emptied the waste baskets, the vacuum cleaner bag, the dryer lint, and the old, rotten vegetables that you neglected in the fridge. Where could you store these bags? In your attic? What happens to that garbage after a few days— or weeks? Does it disappear? Realize that your mind is a similar dumpsite. You cannot store years of resentment, frustration, anger and sadness in bags in your attic. Eventually, the bags will deteriorate, and the odor will permeate your thoughts and actions. You'll find yourself thinking, *I* never would have been allowed to do that. What is *wrong* with her? You'd never catch me talking to *my* parents like that!

As these thoughts and phrases rumble around on the edges of your consciousness, you'll find yourself reacting to things without thinking, repeating comments and negative inferences you heard in childhood, perhaps disguised by today's language. What is the difference between: "you made your bed, so lie in it," and "you made the choice, so deal?" Nothing. The child still hears: "it's your problem, I don't care." It is precisely these types of old, garbage-strewn comments that begin to eat away at the love and trust your child has in you. This is how the disintegration of your relationship with your child begins.

Carrying the trash bags out of the house, resolutely placing them in the hands of your Higher Power, and letting them be disposed of is the necessary action of step 5. Hopefully, becoming the caring parent that you want to be will be the result. Before we begin that work, there is one more inventory area worth considering.

Inventory your own incidents

There is another version of your parenting inventory, which may be relevant for you depending on where you are in the parenting timeline. This is an inventory of your actions as a parent. When have you caused injury or hurt? When have you reacted poorly, irrationally, or have been out of control? Are there decisions or actions you have taken about which you feel guilt or shame? These are items you need to take stock of and then discard. Let's look at how that could be organized, using the same column inventory format we used before.

Incident:	My response:	Affects my:	My part:
I slapped Jamie's leg after he hit me for 3rd time that day. I felt like beating him!	rage, anger, frustration, fear, guilt	self-respect	I lost control of my temper
I held Will down to force him to take medicine – he threw a tantrum. I screamed at him.	rage, frustration, helplessness, remorse	self-esteem	I lost control

In all cases, if you're not comfortable with the column format for your inventory, you may write it out as more of a narrative, e.g.:

I got so mad at Jamie today because he kept hitting me when I told him "no." Finally, the third time he hit me, I lost my temper and hit him back. I slapped him on the leg and he cried. I was so angry that I wanted to keep on hitting him, but I didn't. After I calmed down, I felt so guilty about hitting him, and I felt frustrated and helpless because I hadn't managed to control my own anger.

If you haven't been a parent for very long, or if you have very strong self-control, you may not have much to put on your own personal inventory. This is a good thing! You haven't had time to make too many mistakes yet. If the mistakes are many and your guilt is heavy, you must follow through on this process to release that burden. As before, be "fearless and thorough"! [1]

Another human being

As you've been writing down this list of past transgressions, we assume you are "admitting to yourself" what your responsibility has been. Now comes the hard part. If you haven't yet found a good friend, co-parent, therapist, or spiritual mentor you can confide in, then you need to start looking for one. The fifth step has two parts: recognizing what needs to be disposed of, and trusting God and another human being to help you do the disposing. It's not enough to just admit your errors in judgment to yourself. Sharing them with another person gives you a freedom that you can't find any other way.

Looking for God

We'll re-address the question of God for a moment. Anyone who has given birth, been a witness to a birth, or has adopted a baby and watched him grow into a child, an adolescent, and finally an adult can give voice to the fact that life is a miracle. How impossible it is that all the right brain cells, hormones, muscle groups, bones, and neuronal pathways can collaborate to grow a helpless, incommunicative, wobbly-legged baby into a walking, talking, thinking child who one day becomes a driving, working, loving adult. It's a miracle! Is this a miracle from God the Father of the Torah? Or God the Son from the Gospels? Or God the Higher Power of 12-step programs? Or God the Abundant Spirit of the Universe? Yes, on all counts. I believe so. But it's not what I believe here that will help you with your parenting work. It's *your* belief, understanding, or concept. I believe that "deep down in every man, woman, and child, is the fundamental idea of God,"[2] but I also know that this belief is often difficult to define and even harder to accept. It is necessary here to have at least a *willingness* to believe that a Higher Power exists, and additionally to be open to and honest about including that Power in your self-evaluation so that you will be able to dispose of your trash freely and without reservation. How can you do this?

Yolanda had a difficult time deciding this very issue. She somehow thought that holding on to the guilt and fear she grew up with would help motivate her daughters, age 8 and 11. Her eldest, Tyra, was very mature physically and emotionally. Tyra had grown up without a dad, and at her elementary school, she drifted into a group of girls who were beginning to wear makeup, short skirts, and midriff-baring tee-shirts. Yolanda grew up in a religious home, and believed that children should never talk back or sass their mothers. She had been "backhanded" when she had defiantly complained about her mother's decision to not allow her to date.

Now, she is terrified that her daughter is heading toward an adolescence of sex, drugs and rock n' roll. When we talked about her own early adolescence, Yolanda admitted to sneaking out of her house at night to meet up with a boyfriend whom she was forbidden to see. She said she smoked cigarettes and drank beer starting in seventh grade. Her mother had caught her sneaking back into her room one night, and she had received a well-remembered beating.

Now, when Tyra complains or misbehaves, Yolanda's guilt and fear control her mothering. In essence, she has an unconscious thought process that probably goes something like this:

> *I'm so angry that she's being defiant. I was defiant—I feel guilty that I snuck out of the house. I got a beating that made me hate my mother. I felt guilty about hating her. She was always controlling me. My daughter is controlling me by making me lose my temper. I feel angry about that. And afraid. What if she gets pregnant? What if she's drinking and smoking like I did? I can't let her do that! I can't let her ruin her life!*

The guilt and fear, fed by anger, cause her to make parenting decisions (perhaps beating her own daughter?) that are not led by intelligence or love, or even by instinct, but by *habit*. This is why it's important to take out the trash. Take out these old habits, ingrained from childhood, look at them,

49

read them to someone else whom you know and trust, and then dispose of them!

Yolanda was able to come to a new understanding of the Higher Power she had believed in as a youngster. She re-embraced her childhood religion, and was able to forgive (with a good amount of step work) both her mother and herself for their parenting mistakes. With Jerome, it wasn't so easy.

Jerome grew up in the northeast. His family was hard-working and independent. They lived in a large, metropolitan city, and his parents were both professors at a prestigious university. Although raised culturally as Jewish, the family did not attend religious services, and professed no spiritual beliefs. They loved arguing about politics, philosophy, social injustice, and the need for humanity to "solve our own problems and not wait for some mythical God to do it." Intellectually, Jerome believed that God was unnecessary.

From a young age, Jerome and his dad were very close. Often, they would talk philosophically when they went on fishing trips in the Catskill Mountains. Jerome married and had daughters. His firstborn was sensitive and self-conscious. When Jerome attempted to begin a debate that would have been typical communication in his family of origin, she would either shut down or cry. He was at a loss. He wanted to connect with his girls, but they were so different from him. Jerome was open to the inventory idea; he felt he had already caused some damage to them, as well as to his wife, who was also "sensitive." The only problem was that Jerome knew that there was no God. When we talked about surrender or letting go, Jerome had no idea how to conceive of a higher power. He was stuck.

"How can I surrender to something that is non-existent?" he asked me one day.

"It only has to be a 'power greater than you,'" I quoted.

"I know," he countered, "but the weather is greater than me, I can't control a hurricane or an earthquake, but how is that 'God'? It's a bit difficult to 'believe in' the weather, as people say. I can't really believe that the weather is going to help me learn to be quieter or more sensitive to the needs of my children."

He had a point. I thought for a moment. When were the moments in my life when I felt the presence of God? In prayer and meditation, certainly, but there were also less spiritual times when I had been flooded with a "peace that transcends all understanding,"[3] or when I had the unmistakable yet incomprehensible feeling of confidence that I was safe and loved and taken care of—not due to any human's care, but simply due to an internal sense. This sense, I believe, is God-given. But for Jerome, I phrased it like this:

"Tell me of a time in your life when you felt completely at peace with yourself, your environment, and your life in general."

"I guess the times I felt that most strongly were when my dad and I went fishing in the mountains. I always looked forward to those times when I could just sit in the boat with my line in the lake. We would sit silently together, and all around us it was quiet. I remember having this surreal feeling—yeah, I guess you could call it peace."

"Good!" I emphasized. "Now, do you think, looking back on it, that you manufactured that feeling? Did you create it by your own willpower?"

He smiled ruefully. "No, of course not. It was a feeling that came over me as I sat in the boat. I didn't produce it."

"Right. I think that feeling, peace, is God. Or at least it's a good place to start for you, because that peacefulness is greater than you. You cannot make it appear by your own actions. Sometimes, you'll feel elated or happy because you've done something you enjoy doing, but the peace of the soul is inexplicable."

Jerome was thoughtful for a moment. "How do I surrender to a feeling?"

"Maybe the first step is to create a picture in your mind of what peace is. Maybe it's a picture of that lake where you used to fish. And then, when you have a picture, imagine that Peace gave you the picture and personifies the experience."

"And in the third step prayer, I say, 'I offer myself to Peace'?"

"Yes!"

Jerome's spiritual journey had begun. It can take many years to come to a full understanding of what your Higher Power is. The important part is that you be "willing to grow along spiritual lines." [4]

Admit to God

When you feel you have made a start with this understanding, at least enough to work on the first four steps, it's time to take the next step of trusting God to help you with taking out the trash. The step says to admit "to God, to [your]self and to another human being." The admission to yourself comes mostly through writing down the inventory in step 4. The admission to your Higher Power will come through prayer. It may require some quiet time alone with your inventory, some screaming into a pillow, or some shouting into the waves at the beach. Find the most comfortable way for you to have a conversation with your HP so you can tell Him or Her how angry, let down, and sad you were and are. Then, confess to Him or Her what wrongs or transgressions you committed toward others. Finally, ask that friend, therapist, or spiritual counselor to sit with you so you can read your list aloud. If you wish, you can also just request that this advisor read your inventory silently.

Let it go

Now, it is finally time to take out the trash! This can be as simple and quick as tossing the inventory that you've written into a wastebasket, or it can be a personal, dedicated ritual. I took my trash to the beach, burned it in a bar-b-que grill, and gleefully tossed the ashes into the ocean. As I did the tossing, I said a prayer that I would not take back the hurts, traumas, or bad feelings associated with all of that trash in my life. I made a decision to resolutely turn and face the future as a parent with a clean slate.

Chapter 6

"The most humbling experience—by far—is to be a parent."
~ Denis Prager

The sixth step

I'm now ready to ask my Higher Power to reveal and remove all of my character flaws.

and the seventh step

I will humbly ask Him to remove all of these failings within my character.

Now that you have completed your inventory, have confided in another about your hurts and mistakes, and have hopefully come to an understanding with your Higher Power, it's time to examine the part you play in the parenting drama.

We all have self-inflicted drama in our lives. It comes to us naturally, through our parents, siblings, teachers and any others with whom we have attempted human relationships. It comes from our own character flaws. We react to criticism poorly, or to attention with embarrassment, or to a friend's new dress or video game with envy. It's not new to immerse ourselves in these dramas—to tantrum against the offending person, to cry, whine, beg, or withdraw affection.

It's not new to covet the possessions of another. I can

remember being so envious when Kristy, a single mother friend of mine, received a gift from her new boyfriend of a brand new Big Rider toy car for her son, who was a few months older than Will. Kristy was poor, unemployed, and had a bad relationship with her son's father at the time. I was so envious of her. I was married, living in a house with my husband, the father of my son, but we were on a very tight budget. I knew I couldn't afford the $59 that it cost to buy the bright, fancy toy for Will. I not only sat in this envy, but I entertained it! I told every mom I knew (i.e., I gossiped) that Kristy had no money, was getting food stamps, and that it wasn't right for her to be given such an expensive toy when she had no money for diapers. I told my husband how extravagant her new boyfriend was, how he would spoil her son and then leave her. It would be a bad example for the baby, I said. I assassinated his character without remorse!

It's not unusual to be beset by gluttony, greed, envy, anger, sloth, pride, and lust; admittedly, we have all experienced these "seven deadly sins" (and a few others as well.) But when we become involved with them, consumed by them, the drama that we then invite into our lives and our children's lives can be very damaging.

Take Ben, for example. Ben was raised in an alcoholic home as an only child. His mother, Carol, drank excessively throughout his life, and his father was weak and ineffectual. As a child, Ben was always idealized. Carol enrolled him in the most prestigious schools with the best teachers. Carol signed Ben up for music, art, martial arts, acting lessons, and all the sports teams. Ben auditioned for and received acting and photo modeling jobs as a youngster. His mother emphasized with every action that Ben's worth came from his exterior accomplishments, his appearance, and his ability to be a star. Now, Ben is a self-destructive alcoholic. He is involved with a beautiful, talented woman, but they have an unhappy, combative union. The drama of lust (for power, prestige, and fame) and gluttony (for attention) plays itself out in every aspect of Ben's young adult life. Carol's character flaws have been packaged neatly and given to her son, who will probably continue to act on them with his own children.

The sixth step is a process of admitting and accepting the character flaws that exist within you. You can do this with your inventory in hand, or afterward, in a quiet hour by yourself. Sit with pen and paper, and ask your Higher Power to direct your thinking toward honest self-appraisal. Then, write down each of the character flaws you can identify within yourself. Sometimes, it's helpful to remember that these flaws are evident in all of us, to some extent. We all have failings, and we all act on them without meaning to. The idea here is to get a good look at the ones that are damaging to you and to your relationships with your children.

Below is a list of the more common character flaws, and examples of how they have manifested themselves in the lives of some of the parents I've known. These imperfections flourished in their lives, and they became ineffective (and sometimes very damaging) parenting attitudes:

Sue   **Gluttony/stinginess**: I hated sharing when I was a child. My parents never allowed us to save our Halloween candy or other treats. We ate some of the candy on Halloween, and then it was thrown away. When we had dessert or treats, we always had to divide it up evenly, and my father always got the extra share, since he was the bread-winner, I guess. I never felt that there was enough for me. Now, when my child overeats or takes candy or toys from others, I get extremely agitated. I hate it when he won't share. When he hoards candy or other treats in his room, I go

ballistic. I can't seem to help myself;
I have even taken candy from his
room and eaten it!

Kate **Greed/covetousness**: There was
never enough money in our home to
buy new, expensive toys. We were
told to "make do with what we had."
My mom sewed my clothes, or went
to the secondhand sale at church. We
hardly ever had new things. I work
really hard to earn a good living, and
I buy myself things on sale or at
discount stores. My clothes are nice,
but not extravagant. When my
daughter wants a new brand-name
outfit, I get upset with her. I told her
the other night that she was a selfish,
spoiled brat. Then I felt horrible
afterward. I can't seem to stop saying
negative things to her.

Anelle **Envy/jealousy**: I was so envious of
my friend Bonnie when I was
growing up. She had a pink bedroom,
a dog, and a cool, young mom. She
also seemed to make friends easily,
unlike me. I always wanted to be just
like her. In fact, I wanted to *be* her.
My daughter, Sam, is insecure and
nervous. I keep taking her to ballet
classes, Brownies, and soccer. I want
her to be a joiner. She complains that
she doesn't like all the activities, but
I'm determined: she's not going to be
a lonely wallflower like me!

Seth **Anger/impatience**: My dad was

angry and impatient about everything. Once, he threw my books across the room because I was being "obstinate and lazy," when in fact, I just didn't understand the chemistry problems. The other day, when I was trying to get my 2-year-old to preschool, I yelled: "come on, we have to go *now!*" and grabbed his hand to drag him out the doorway. He stomped his foot and said "walk self!" I laughed at his cute self-assertion, but then I realized how impatient I was being— just like my dad!

Andy **Sloth/laziness**: I think I've been depressed my whole life. Some mornings, I hate waking up. Life is so hard. I work hard at my job, but the rest of my life is a total mess. I even gave up seeing my 4-year-old son. I know I should go and visit him on the weekends, but I've just been avoiding it, I guess.

Keiko **Pride/arrogance**: My mother and father both worked all the time when I was growing up. We had a lot of things that other kids didn't have, like a new car every year. I went to a prestigious school and was popular. I got straight A's, and was in tons of activities. My dad always said that we were "better than other people" because we were smart. What we really were was perfectionistic. My ex used to tell me all the time that I was too good for everyone.

The other day, I heard my 7-year-old bragging to her friends that we had a new DVD player and surround sound because we were rich. It sounded so awful! I've also noticed recently that she throws a fit and tears up drawings or papers she's worked on because they're "not perfect." She seems to be confident on the outside, but I know how lonely it feels to be so driven to perfection.

Jon   **Lust/neediness**: I grew up in two cultures; mom was Korean, and Dad was Spanish. I went to boarding school in Spain from the time I was about 12. When Dad died, I was 20, and I took over the family business. I lived in Seoul with my mom for two years, but her ideas about how to live drove me crazy. Eventually, I hooked up with an amazing, wild girl and we took off for Europe. We had a great time sailing, gambling, drinking, clubbing. Somewhere along the line, I started doing drugs, too. Our relationship was totally indulgent, and I guess it was self-destructive, too. It ended when I went into rehab last year to clean up my act.

I met Suzanne when I was newly recovering. She has helped me straighten out. She's a great girl, and has never been into the drug scene. At first, we did a lot of fun things together. When I proposed, I flew her to Madrid for a long weekend! Now, she's seven months pregnant and I want to get married, but all we've been doing is fighting. She gets so jealous when I watch porn or look at other women. She won't go out with me and our friends anymore because she says she's too "fat." I just want to enjoy my life with her. I wish we could have sex and fool around like we used to. She's never in the mood. She's never there for me.

Your list of character flaws may contain some or all of those listed above. Certainly, some of these examples are extreme, and it's easy to see how these flaws could adversely affect the raising of children, but even when they are minor, don't our flaws cause us, and therefore our children, harm? How many of you, when you had your first glimpse of your precious newborn, said to yourselves: "well, if I pass down a few of my minor character flaws, that's ok, as long as I don't teach him to steal…"

Humbly ask Him to remove all of these failings

Once you have created your own list of flaws, spend a few quiet moments with your Higher Power. You may even want to set it aside for a day or two, so you can allow your awareness to open up. Sometimes, God will reveal things to you that are buried. When this happens, just add them to your list, and thank Him for helping you become the best parent (and person) you can be.

If you're satisfied that this step is through, proceed to the seventh step. The reason that this step requires humility is clear: we have to admit we are flawed, imperfect creatures. We have to come spirit-to-spirit with our Creator, and ask to be forgiven for indulging in these flaws to the extent that we have. This is a private conversation to have with your Higher Power. The traditional "7th Step Prayer"[1] from the book

Alcoholics Anonymous may be useful:

> My Creator,
>
> I am now willing that
>
> You should have all of me,
>
> Good and bad.
>
> I pray that you now remove from me
>
> Every single defect of character which
>
> Stands in the way of my usefulness
>
> To you and my fellows.
>
> Grant me strength,
>
> As I go out from here,
>
> To do your bidding.
>
> Amen.

It is helpful, too, to repeat this prayer with your children's names:

"I am now willing that you should have all of _____, good and bad. I pray that you now remove from him/her every single defect of character which stands in the way of his/her usefulness to you . . ."

As with the first three, the seventh step requires a commitment of surrender, humility, and faith that there is Someone there who can actually take that trash bag full of bad memories, mistakes, and personal failings—and remove it from you.

Chapter 7

"Our real purpose is to fit ourselves to be of maximum service to God and the people about us."

~ *Alcoholics Anonymous*

The eighth step

I'm willing to have my Higher Power reveal to me anyone I have harmed.

and the ninth step

I'm willing to make amends to whomever I have hurt.

Are there people in your past to whom you owe an apology? Were you the kind of teenager who gave your mother gray hair? Did you steal cigarettes from your Dad and "borrow" the car while he was asleep? Perhaps you committed more heinous acts that you know you need to atone for.

One dad I know cut school, smoked cigarettes and pot, and drank beer almost daily in the last two years that he was in high school. Sad to say, he didn't graduate from high school, and it took him several years to find the path back to a productive life. Now, he's a dad of two young boys. He constantly makes reference to "when they're teenagers" in a joking, yet apprehensive, way. This dad told me he feels his sons are "doomed to repeat the same things I did." Is this repetition compulsory? Are our teens sentenced to repeat our mistakes? Certainly, our news media and sociologists who study popular culture tell us that teenagers are bound to be— almost required to be—rebellious, angry, sullen, disrespectful, non-communicative, anti-authority and even felonious!

In the book *Preparing your Son for Every Man's Battle*, authors Arterburn and Stoeker assert that:

> A sociologist, if devoid of God's absolute truth, is really little more than a news anchor reporting what he sees in the world every day. What he reports is no more the truth than the repeated horrors on our daily newscasts prove that we all live in a perpetual state of catastrophe and violence. Yet we are told to expect that same behavior from our own teens, and when our children turn twelve, we start to cower before the adolescent years. [1]

They state, and I agree, that our children (and their parents) are granted free will by our Creator. You can use this free will to continue the patterns that caused you harm and distress in your childhood, or to change direction and open up a new path for your children to travel upon. This is the freedom to let go of generations of inherited parenting flaws. In great part, this letting go is an act of conscious decision by you, the parent. Completing this mental and emotional housecleaning is the key to readiness.

So far, you have surrendered your control and management of your child. You have turned your own will and your child's will over to the care of God, as you understand Him or Her. You have written down all the parenting "wrongs" that were perpetrated against you by the parents and adults in your own life, and by you to your own children. You have shared this inventory, and made admissions of your own character flaws and mistakes. What a lot of work! This next part is a breeze by comparison.

It is between you and your HP. The important thing is to be willing to place yourself in the position of being humble before Him or Her. Humility has been defined as the state of modesty, or meekness, but I was taught that humility is the state of being "teachable." Ask yourself if you're ready to learn from God how, when, and who you have affected in a harmful way. Consider quietly, in communion with your Higher Power: to whom do I owe amends? When have I caused harm, hurt feelings, or been unfaithful, angry, or even malicious? To whom do you want me to make amends?

Those to whom you owe amends will probably be listed in your fourth step inventory, and many do this step (and steps 6 and 7) directly after reading the inventory to the "other human being" you chose. This ensures that you remember all of your transgressions. If you do not have the inventory to consult, simply spend time in prayer and thought. There may be several people with whom you want to set things right. Before you take any action, write all of the names on a list. Consider the importance and validity of each entry. For example:

Dad ~   I misbehaved; thought he was too old fashioned and conservative. Hated him; got drunk on his cognac, dropped out of college, was disrespectful. Didn't talk to him for two years because I was angry.

Step Mom ~   Made her life miserable. Blamed her for everything. Held grudges, argued, was disrespectful every day. Stole money from her purse to buy cigarettes.

Friend, Ali ~   Dated her boyfriend behind her back. Cheated with him and never told her. I was jealous of her and insecure. Gossiped about her to other friends.

There is a contemporary idea that guilt is bad; it is a

negative emotion, and, like shame, should be abolished. You should never make your kids feel guilty; neither should you feel guilty. Just do what you have to do and don't feel guilty. I submit that this may be a dangerous attitude for a parent. It may be even more dangerous for you to pass along this attitude to your kids.

> D.W. Winnicott, noted psychiatrist and child development expert, talked about the 'vital role in human development of the growth of a healthy capacity to experience guilt...He made it plain that a capacity to experience guilt is a necessary attribute of the healthy person.'[2]

Because of the power of guilt, we feel bad. Our consciences hurt. We are uncomfortable. When thus discomfited, we can ignore, bury, or deny our feelings, or we can clear our consciences by making amends to others. Often, we are too ashamed to do the latter. This sense of shame can be deep, and it can have its roots in early development. Look at the case of Danielle.

Danielle was a darling, curly-haired, bright child who was adopted by a doting but neurotic and infertile mother. Her adoptive father was caring, but he was absent with work and passivity. Danielle's mother was, in turns, adoring and pushy or critical and remonstrative. When she drank, which was increasingly often as Danielle entered middle school, her mother became cruel and mean-spirited. If Danielle was in the school play, her mother clapped the loudest, bragged the most, and praised her daughter lavishly. But if Danielle brought home a poor grade, wasn't invited to a popular child's party, or received a less-than-stellar review from a teacher or coach, her mother became abusive, screaming things like, "you'll never amount to anything," or "you can't do anything right." Even, at times, "I wish I'd never adopted you."

Very early in her life, probably when she was in the late infant stage of Separation and Individuation (a term first used and described by Dr. Margaret Mahler, one of the first developmental theorists), which happens when a child is about 12 to 18 months old, Danielle developed an overwhelming sense of shame. When a child is very young, she cannot tolerate believing that she is "bad, evil, or wicked." And yet, if her mother is the one telling her these things, she knows they must be true, so the part of her that hears and believes this harsh assessment must be subverted. It is too dangerous for her to believe that she is bad, and it is even more dangerous in her infant's cognitive belief system to believe that her mother is bad. What happens is that she splits off the part of herself that she finds bad or unacceptable to her mother and herself; henceforth, she denies it even exists. Internally, the unconscious dialog goes something like this:

▸ Mother says I am bad when I whine or cry.
Mother yells and shuts me in my room.
Mother hurts and rejects me. I hate Mother.

▸ I can't hate Mother. She is everything. She feeds me, changes me and cares for me. She is my life.

▸ I must be bad. I can't be bad. If I am bad, Mother will abandon me. I have to get rid of the badness. I will throw it away.

This throwing away or splitting off parts of the self is the origin of shame. Shame is the knowledge that "I am wrong." I am wrong because my mother finds me unacceptable. Guilt, by contrast, is the knowledge that "I've done wrong." This is a very important distinction. If we are fully acceptable to our parents, we do not fall into shame. If we are not shamed, we are able to tolerate the idea and knowledge that we have done wrong. And if we can admit we've done wrong, we can make it right. This theory is authenticated by the *Diagnostic and Statistical Manual of the American Psychiatric Association IV*. This foundational tome lists the "absence of guilt"[3] as one of the symptoms of the serious mental disorder known as Antisocial Personality Disorder. Without guilt, how are we motivated to go back and apologize if we've hurt a friend's feelings? Or disappointed a parent? Or done wrong to another? How do we know if we've done wrong to our child? It's the guilt—the gift that keeps on giving, as my friend Lori says.

Yes, guilt is a negative emotion, but it's the "capacity for feeling guilt [that] implies the tolerance of ambivalence and an acceptance of responsibility for both our love and our hate."[4] To the extent that we can feel the weight of our misdeeds, we acquire the humility to confess them and the courage to make them right. We are then freed of their weight and begin to experience the joy of life.

Therefore, feel the guilt and the freedom that comes from flaws and failures, attributes and good deeds, resentments and jubilations. It is the ambivalence of our lives that marks us as humans. It's our inability to tolerate that ambivalence that brings us to our knees to ask God to help us.

I'm willing to have my Higher Power reveal to me anyone I have harmed

Once you have created your amends list, consider setting it aside for a day or two to allow time for more incidents to come to light. This list shouldn't be a second inventory, but an echo of the first. List only names and brief, pertinent details. Prayerfully consider who and what you need to put on this list.

One parent I know had a chaotic upbringing. Her parents were extremely permissive, allowing Elaine and her siblings to drink and smoke pot in the house with their friends, and implicitly condoning their sexual activity. Elaine was only 14 when she developed a serious crush on her older brother's friend named Alex. They "partied" in Elaine's home together, and one night during some heavy petting, Alex convinced her to show him her bedroom. They were intoxicated, but Elaine remembered telling him "no," and asking him to "stop" to no avail. The next day, she confided to her mother, who told her she had "asked for it" and she "should have known better" than to ask him upstairs. No one else in the family acknowledged the incident. She became pregnant from this rape, and her mother took her to the clinic where she aborted the fetus. Her mother advised her to "forget about the whole thing. Just put it behind you." She never talked about it again with anyone.

Elaine told this story to me with tears in her eyes, thirty years later. It had been the catalyst that changed her adolescence. By 15, she was drinking every weekend and had a different boyfriend every week. She had several more abortions, enrolled in and dropped out of several colleges, and went deeper into addiction as the years passed. Her parents bailed her out of jail for drunk driving offenses several times. They gave her money for abortions, new starts, vehicles, and rehabs. She never held a steady job, and when she was destitute, she always returned home, where she would rail against her parents for being the worst parents in the world.

Elaine wasn't sure whether to put her parents on her amends list. Even though she was clean and sober now, and had done a lot of therapeutic work, she still harbored a great deal of anger and resentment about the way they had raised her. She was still angry that her mother had been so cold when she was raped. Her trauma had been real, and healing from it wasn't complete. I told Elaine that she had to ask God about what to do.

A few days later, she told me she had decided to include them on her amends list. "They weren't the best parents. They didn't give me what I needed as a teenager, and I'm still angry about that. But I wasn't a good daughter either. I decided to make amends for my part in the relationship, and leave the rest up to them."

Amends to your children

As indicated by your inventory list, you may have included your own children on your amends list. If you have been a parent for awhile, you certainly have incidents about which you feel guilty or remorseful. If you are certain that they will understand the process, and that it will benefit them, make amends to them directly.

Will ~ Forced medicine down his throat. Became angry when he spit it back out.

Became angry and frustrated with him when he wouldn't participate during "Mommy and Me" time.

These incidents happened with Will when he was a toddler. I see the benefit of admitting them to someone else (fifth step) and to my Higher Power now, because I still have remorse about them. I also see the benefit of seeing my own character flaws inherent within these lapses in good parenting. I do not see the benefit, for either Will or me, to go to him now, as a teenager, and tell him that I am sorry for something that happened between us when he was two years old. If we're ever in a discussion that warrants inclusion of this information, I will certainly use it, but for now, I can decide to make amends silently, by being a better parent on a daily basis. This is a living amends: I live up to the standard of my decisions as fully and honestly as I can.

I'm willing to make amends

The actual process of the ninth step is simple. What it requires is willingness and humility. Elaine decided to write a card to her parents so that she wouldn't be tempted to get into finger-pointing and blaming, which was another family trait that she didn't want to continue. Her card was simple; it read:

Mom and Dad,

Thank you for supporting me in the current college classes I'm taking. I'd like to become self-supporting in this next year. I sincerely apologize to you both for taking financial advantage of you for so long. Also, I'm sorry for the times I have caused you worry or distress. I love you,

Elaine

Her parents received this note, but they never commented upon it or offered amends to her for the hurts they had caused her over the years. Nevertheless, she reported to me a sense of lightness and freedom that she hadn't experienced before. She felt, for the first time, that she could let go of "all that childhood stuff" and become the kind of mother to her children that she wanted to be.

Perhaps not everyone on your list will truly need you to make amends. For example, take my violin teacher. Had I broken her violin, set her music books on fire, or somehow gotten her fired from the school, perhaps I would have needed to make concrete amends to her. As it was, I held onto childish hatred and resentment every time I saw her in the hallways. I made fun of the way she dressed, and I made fun of her poor son who was in my class. While not demonstrative of the most mature or desirable behavior, this is hardly the stuff that requires amends. The test is this: did my actions cause her pain or anguish? And does the memory of those actions contribute to or detract from my parenting work? If the answer to the first question is yes, then I'm obliged to make an attempt at contacting her to apologize. The second question is really for my self-evaluation; it provides insight for me to use in my parenting work. My son took violin for a year. When he wanted to quit, I had to discuss it with my husband, and emotionally separate my experience from my son's. Had I had a parenting "sponsor" or mentor, I could have discussed it with her.

If making amends will cause harm

When making amends will cause harm to someone, do not proceed. In the sample list on page 65, I included a friend whom I harmed without her knowledge. She never found out that her boyfriend cheated with me. If I told her now, it would not make things right between us. In fact, I haven't even seen Ali since high school. To call her now and hurt her feelings about a betrayal that is long past would be cruel and unnecessary. Better that I make amends with my Higher Power, ask His or Her forgiveness, and let it go.

Amends can be made in person, on the phone, or by letter. If you cannot locate someone of whom you need to ask forgiveness, you can make amends by journaling and sharing the journal entry with a trusted friend or sponsor. There are other creative ways of completing this process. Write a note, tear it up and toss it into the fireplace; do a role-play with someone you trust; do whatever it takes to feel that you have satisfied your own internal guilt.

The last form of making amends is in the way that you choose to live. If your parent was angry, aggressive or punitive, you can choose to change that pattern in your interactions with your child. You can be kind where you were treated cruelly, supportive where you were criticized, respectful where you were disrespected. In the end, the amends you make by living this way are to yourself. In becoming a kind, supportive, respectful person, you are able to treat yourself in similar manner, and thus free yourself from the bondage of your own childhood.

I have always liked the prayer of St. Francis of Assisi, [5] as it offers the hope of righting all those wrongs that we carry still inside of us:

Lord, make me an instrument of your peace.
Where there is hatred, let me sow love;
Where there is injury, pardon;
Where there is doubt, faith;
Where there is despair, hope;
Where there is darkness, light;
And where there is sadness, joy.

O divine Master, grant that I may not so much seek
To be consoled as to console;
To be understood as to understand;
To be loved as to love.
For it is in giving that we receive,
It is in pardoning that we are pardoned,
And it is in dying that we are born to eternal life.

Part III — Seek

"There is a principle which is a bar against all information, which is proof against all arguments and which cannot fail to keep a man in everlasting ignorance—that principle is contempt prior to investigation."

~ Herbert Spencer

Chapter 8

"As you have the light, believe in the light. Then the light will be within you, and shining through your lives. You'll be children of the light."

~ The Message; John 12:36

The tenth step

I will continue to take daily inventory, and when I'm wrong, promptly admit it.

Continue to take daily inventory

"My toddler cries every time I come home. He's fine for the nanny. As soon as I'm out of sight, he stops crying, she says. But when I come home, he begins the whining and wailing. He pulls at my pants leg, wanting me to pick him up immediately." My client, a weary mother of two kids under age 4, was asking me: "Should I give in to him?"

"What do you mean by 'give in to'?" I asked.

"Well, my girlfriend says that when he cries and whines, he's trying to manipulate me and I shouldn't give in to him."

"So, 'giving in to him' means picking him up?"

"Yes, and letting him have his own way."

"In my view, you're asking me if you should comfort your small son who is verbalizing his needs to you. He's telling you that it was difficult for him to be away from you. He's expressing his feelings about your separation."

"Oh, so it's ok to comfort him?"

Yes!

He's not manipulating or controlling you. Can you even imagine being controlled by a 2-foot-5-inch toddler who cannot even talk yet? In fact, some parents can. One well-intentioned grandparent told me that my 6-week-old infant was "working me" by his fairly constant colicky fussing every night. "He's conditioning you to pick him up," was the dispassionate observation. "You'll spoil him if you keep it up."

It's not really a parent's imagination that her newborn baby is crying "on purpose" to force her to pick him up! In a sense, he is. A baby cries "on purpose" because it has needs; for example, a baby needs love, warmth, food, comfort, drink, dry clothing, physical and intellectual stimulation. These needs all make a baby cry. Crying is the only method the baby has to communicate its needs. When the needs are met, by the parent picking up the baby and attending to the need, the baby usually stops crying. This is not spoiling a baby, nor is it the baby manipulating the parent. It is the way God ensures that the baby's needs will receive a proper response.

This need-provision continues on in a child's life until he or she is nearly an adult. At some point, of course, the child begins to be clearer about verbalizing his or her needs, and at that same point, a parent (hopefully) begins to distinguish between a child's true needs and wants. This distinction usually begins when the baby starts to "talk" and can ask for things, like lollipops, by pointing or using rudimentary words. The parent then begins to teach the child in subtle ways how to differentiate: "No, Pammy, you don't need a lollipop—here, if you're hungry, how about some yummy raisins?"

In time, a child is able to provide what she needs, and much of what she wants, for herself. The ability of the child to take care of herself, i.e., to provide for her own needs, is mostly dependent upon whether the child's needs are met in those early days and months, when her sleep-deprived, distracted, trying-to-take-care-of-business parents are nearly destroyed by the invasion of a new being in their previously calm and orderly lives. If these parents are able to provide for the most basic of her needs, and thereby teach her that she is worthy of having them met, she will eventually come to provide for them herself.

What this has to do with taking a "daily inventory" you may well be wondering. Let me answer that with another story.

James, who is 13 and struggling to adjust to the rapid onset of adolescent hormones conflicting with his dependent, second-born, and sweetly affectionate natural personality, just came into my office and asked me if I wanted to watch a T.V. show with him. My first response: no, I'm busy (working on the computer.) After a few seconds of hesitation, I felt guilty, then resentful—he's *making* me feel guilty. Guilt always brings on a feeling of annoyance for me. I just want it to go away so that I can go on doing what *I* want to do. It's like a buzzing mosquito. I kept typing away, but there was the guilt buzzing around and around. So annoying.

I was about to say something more to James about how he should understand that I have to work sometimes, when my intellect took over and I thought: wait—no one can *make* me feel anything. I feel guilty because this is my boy, asking to spend time with me, and I'm being selfish and don't want to be distracted. Then I thought: hmmm—he's a teenager; for him, these moments of desired closeness are farther and farther apart. But right this very minute, he's asking for something he needs: closeness with me. Do I want to let that pass? No. I want to be responsive when I can. I want to keep our relationship as close as he'll let me. This was my on-the-spot "daily" inventory.

It's not as complicated as it sounds. It's a matter of developing an observing conscience, or "observing ego," as psychiatrist Carl Jung called it. Simply put, it's the part of your mind that's aware of the existence and thoughts in other parts of your consciousness. Let's look at it this way. If I'm angry, upset, frustrated, guilty, or any of several other negative emotions, and I ignore the reality of that emotion, it will affect me and my parenting work adversely. I'll become resentful and react to my kids in a negative way. Faber and Mazlish put it this way: "Sounding patient when I'm feeling angry can only work against me. Not only do I fail to communicate honestly, but because I've been 'too nice,' I wind up letting it out on my child later on."[1]

So, rather than swallow my own emotion, I process it, on the spot, in my head. Am I obligated to do what I'm doing? Does this work have a deadline I'm committed to? Is my need to keep working because of an old voice in my head that says I'll "spoil" my children if I do what they want me to do? Or is it truly my own value that says I really need to work right now, and my child will adjust? If it's the latter, I can say to James, "you know, sweetheart, I'd like to watch your program with you, but I have to work right now. Can we play cards together later on?" He may or may not agree to this, but at least he has a chance of feeling acknowledged instead of ignored.

Kids have lots of feelings

He may say: "You never play with me anymore," which I can now hear as "I really miss you." If I'm feeling guilty and resentful, I hear that statement as "you're a bad mommy," but if I've taken my mini-inventory, I realize that he's expressing his feelings. It's not about me. How can I tell the difference? That's fairly simple with kids. It's almost never about me. Babies, kids, teenagers, young adults—even us "older" adults—our statements are almost always about ourselves and our own feelings. How many times have you said to your partner, wife, boyfriend, sister, or child any of these things:

> ✔ "**You** never do the dishes."
>
> ✔ "Why don't **you** ever throw your clothes in the hamper instead of on the floor?"
>
> ✔ "**We** have to do something about that faucet."
>
> ✔ "**She's** so gross. Look at **her** belly button sticking out."

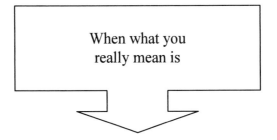

When what you
really mean is

> ✔ "**I'm** so tired of washing the dishes; **I wish** you'd do them."
>
> ✔ "I don't like having dirty underwear on the floor."
>
> ✔ "**I hate** listening to the faucet drip. I want you to fix it for me."
>
> ✔ "I feel so worried that you'll dress like her, attract the wrong kind of boy and get in trouble!"

Can you imagine what our families would be like if we all communicated our needs and wants clearly, expressing our needs instead of camouflaging them with statements that are sometimes attacking, often inflammatory, and almost always confusing to others?

Let's look at this in the context of how we interpret our kids' feelings for a moment. Our children have strong emotions, and often they have not developed the "filter" that softens their demands, worries, and incessant wants. It can be like that guilt mosquito, buzzing around and around in the parent's head: I want - I need - I want. So often the parent feels compelled to do or provide what the child is asking for. This isn't always the best thing for the child; obviously, we shouldn't provide every desired candy bar, trip to the movies, or new gadget that our children want.

Alternatively, a parent might become irritated at the constant barrage of requests and deny his child every wish. This can be discouraging for both the child and the parent. The parent isn't allowed the gratification of seeing his child enjoy something, and the child is constantly frustrated in his desires. So what is the best course of action?

There are two tasks here. The first one is to tune your ears to hear the child's feelings that are being expressed just beneath his or her statements. The second task is to identify your own feelings and separate them from the ones your kid is going through so that you can respond in a non-reactive way. This sounds complicated, but you'll see how simple it can be. On the next page, there are a few examples that may sound familiar. In the second box, I've listed some alternative statements that may be closer to what the child is actually feeling. Can you see how easy it would be to react negatively to the statements in the first box? But if your child were able to say the secondary statements instead, wouldn't it change your response?

- "I hate my brother. He's such a thief!"

- "Why don't you just throw out all of my clothes? You never let me wear anything that's cool!"

- "Mom, don't get out of the car when you drop me off at school."

- "Why can't I go to the mall? You're so lame!"

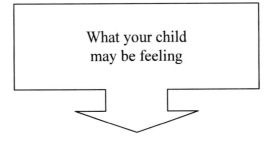

What your child
may be feeling

- "I'm angry that my brother took my I-Pod without asking!"

- "I want to fit in with my friends. I feel really insecure."

- "I'm embarrassed because you keep hugging me in front of all of my friends."

- "I feel so smothered! I just want to be with my peers."

Parents have feelings, too

You may not like the feelings beneath these statements. They may even engender some negative feelings in you. This is precisely why the tenth step is so important. We parents need to keep track of our own feelings, regulate them, process them, and then decide how to act in response to our kids' feelings. That is, we need to *act* instead of *react*! That is a tall order.

So often, I react without conscious intent in ways that hurt my children. Our feelings (theirs and mine) are so intricately connected that it's often hard for me to separate them. If I had said to James, for example, "You never let me finish my work!" or "Why are you pestering me again?" his feelings would have been hurt, he might have felt embarrassed and angry, and he would have then reacted to my reaction. His reaction would most likely have been one that got my attention in a negative way. Misbehavior is the most common form of revenge. When kids can't or won't express their anger or hurt, they misbehave instead.

What a cycle we create when we speak without thinking! As adults, we must use our filter; we must not react before thinking.

On the next pages, there are two possible scenarios for my conversation with James. There could be other conversations, too, each with its own potential for miscommunication. Look at each of the ones I've shown, and notice the possible feelings present. James' comments are in boldfaced type; mine are indented, in plain type. In the parentheses, I've identified possible feelings.

✔ **Mommy, do you want to watch a show with me?**

(James: desire for closeness)

> Not right now, sweetie, I'm working on the computer.
>
> (Me: work pressure)

✔ **You're always working!**

(James: not heard, frustrated)

> That's because I need to make money to buy you all the things you want!
>
> (Me: guilt, frustration, diverting blame)

✔ **I don't want to buy things. That's Will. He's the one always wanting stuff.**

(James: resentment—Mom is making excuses, blaming me.)

> OK, whatever! I need to work. Please stop pestering me.
>
> (Me: losing patience; don't want to deal with his emotions)

✔ **You never play with me . . .** (some scuffling noises) **OWWW! Flower!** (our dog) **Stop it! OWWWWW!**

(James: not heard, angry, getting revenge for Mom's blame)

> James! Go watch your show! Come on! I mean it!
>
> (Me: angry, impatient)

✔ **You're so mean! You don't even care that Flower scratched me!** (slams office door)

(James: angry, uncared for)

> (muttering) What a pain in the neck.
>
> (Me: angry, resentful)

✔ **Mommy, do you want to watch a show with me?**

(James: desire for closeness)

> Not right now, sweetie, I'm working on the computer.
>
> (Me: work pressure)

✔ **You're always working!**

(James: not heard, frustrated)

> I know, it sure seems that way, huh?
>
> (Me: guilt, frustration, trying to listen for his feelings)

✔ **It *is* that way! You never want to play with me!**

(James: resentful, frustrated)

> Sounds like you miss me.
>
> (Me: tuning in, instead of avoiding his feelings)

✔ **Yeah, I guess.**

(James: heard, understood)

> I miss you too. I wish I had more time to play.
>
> (Me: tuning in, instead of avoiding my feelings)

✔ **Well, maybe after dinner we can play backgammon?**

(James: cared for, able to offer a solution)

> What a great idea. Right after dinner, then.
>
> (Me: relieved, peaceful)

Isn't it amazing how differently these two conversations conclude? The only real difference between the first and second scenarios is that in the first, I'm able to tune into his feelings, separate my own from his, and then attend to him directly. The difference seems small, but the outcome is significant. In one, we end up as enemies, at odds over a simple request on his part that has escalated into his angry misbehavior (slamming the door and yelling at both me and the dog) and my frustration and anger at him. In the other conversation, we are able to say our disappointments, admit that we miss each other and want to spend time together, and come to a solution that suits both of us. When you think about how many of these interactions you have with your child in a day or week—over his or her entire childhood—what an impact this can have!

Separating my feelings from my child's feelings. This is the challenge. How am I able to achieve this as an on-the-spot mommy miracle? The answer is simple: I practice a lot. I don't do it perfectly, but there are many opportunities to work on it. I spend lots of time listening. I try to hold back on my reactions to clearly hear what my boys are saying to me. If necessary, I can even delay my reaction for several hours. I can say: "I don't have a good answer for you right now. Let me think about it, and I'll get back to you later. This allows me the space to look at my feelings (and theirs) with a detached eye.

If the instant processing method isn't effective, I can do a tenth step inventory on paper. I prepare it much the same as my fourth step inventory:

Incident:	My response:	Affects my:
James pestered me	blamed and scolded him for interrupting me	self-worth as a mom

At times, I have been so overwhelmed with the feelings of motherhood that I've had to do a written tenth step daily, just to clean out my attic, so that in the morning, I could start with a fresh attitude. It's very hard when the feelings that my child has are so deeply enmeshed with the feelings that I have. The nightly inventory allows me to step back, realize my parenting mistakes, and see how I could have handled things better. As my dear friend Fran used to say, "the thing about kids is they'll always give you another chance to practice your parenting skills." I know that I'll have another chance to make things right by doing it differently. Probably tomorrow.

When I'm wrong, promptly admit it

Whether I'm writing a formal tenth step at night or performing an on-the-spot one when I'm in the midst of a feeling-storm, it's important that I evaluate my part in the situation and make amends when needed. I can either add a "my part" column to my written inventory, or I can mentally account for it.

Incident:	My response:	Affects my:	My part:
James pestered me I was impatient	I blamed and scolded him for interrupting me	self worth as a mom	I didn't think things through; felt remorse

At this point, I can go to James and make amends. I can tell him: "I'm sorry I yelled at you yesterday when you wanted me to watch T.V. with you." He'll usually say, "It's OK, Mom, don't worry about it." I could also add to this some corrective actions: "Will you give me another chance to spend time with you?" This does two things. It shows him that I really mean what I say, and it teaches him how to make amends. My actions can be such a powerful teaching tool.

The key to the tenth step is the ability for you to separate and set aside your feelings so that you can attend to your child's. Your ability to tune in is impaired on a daily basis by your own long-ago unmet needs, unfulfilled desires, fears and wants, as well as by current life stressors, pressures and requirements that you must address. Your tuner is worn down, and even broken in certain spots, because of these old injuries and current stresses. In order to repair and restore your tuner, you need your Higher Power. As you know, only your Higher Power can "restore you to sanity;" so, too, your HP can repair your tuner.

Chapter 9

"God will constantly disclose more to you and to us."

~ *Alcoholics Anonymous*

The eleventh step

I will seek through prayer and meditation to improve my conscious contact with God, *as I understand Him,* praying only for knowledge of His will for me and my kids and the power to carry that out.

I want it!

It's difficult when I'm standing in line at the grocery store, trying to check out, and my child is nagging, over and over, *"I want candy. I want caaaandy. I want caaannnndyy. I waaaannnntttt caaaannnnddddyyyy."* At that precise moment, were it not for the 20 other people standing in line nearby, I would start to scream and jump up and down and whine: *"I want a child who doesn't drive me craaaaazzzyyy!"* It's difficult to summon the spiritual awareness, peace and calm to quietly say: "I need you to stop asking for candy now," or "I wish you would be quiet for a moment," or better still: "Boy, you sure do love candy!"

Most of us eventually resort to "reason" in these moments: "You can't have candy now, because we're having dinner as soon as we get home," or bargaining: "if you stop asking now, you can have a candy bar after dinner tonight," or even threats: "If you ask me for candy again, there'll be no dessert for you tonight." These techniques work with varying success. Sometimes they result in even bigger arguments, louder whining, and more uncontrollable behavior. There are a couple of ways to abate this child's candy wish. The most effective may be the brief explanation attached to a statement that shows you understand the child's feeling: "You know, it's not candy time right now. But I sure hear how much you want some!" This may be followed by the question: "Why isn't it candy time?" or the assertion: "I say it *is* candy time."

To either of these, you may reply, simply, "you wish it were time for candy." When the child begins to pester for more information, it's her way of saying: "If I keep this conversation going, I'll be able to get what I want." (There is no need to continue to reason with or explain the situation to your child. You have already supplied the reason once. Do not repeat it in the vain hope that she will hear your explanation and suddenly give up.) Now you are free to continue addressing her feelings. "You really want—," or "You'd like it if—," or even "boy, you sure love candy!" Your child may have more feelings than you can tolerate due to your own worn down "tuner" as we discussed. You may finally just reduce your own need to respond. Try a simple reply of "hmmm" or "oh," to let your child know you are still listening, but are not going to change your mind.

Nancy was an older mom. She had two girls, aged 3 and 6. She had waited a long time to marry, and she had such a great desire to have children and be a stay-at-home mom that she imagined parenting would come "naturally" to her. She was mistaken. Her first child, Grace, was verbal and bright. Grace bonded with her easily, she felt, and was a good, easygoing baby. When Grace was 2, Nancy was pregnant with Mia. When Mia was first born, Grace was very happy to "play Mama" to the baby. She helped Nancy change the baby and rock her to sleep. Within a few weeks, Grace began exhibiting some testing behavior. If they all went to the local shopping mall for lunch, Grace wouldn't stay in the stroller. She would hop out and run away. When they were in a store, Grace would hide under the clothing racks and Nancy would panic, trying to find her. But the worst part of the shopping trips was the constant whining. Grace would beg and plead for treats, candy, or toys whenever they were shopping. The pleading went on and on until Nancy either gave in to her or lost her temper. In either case, Nancy ended up feeling like the worst mother in the world. "When I give in to her, I know I'm spoiling her, but I hate yelling at her, and I can't get her to stop asking otherwise. What else can I do?" she asked me at a parent meeting.

Not every parent is suited for every child. Many times, a child's need to express her feelings is greater, longer, louder, and more persistent than a parent's ability to hear that expression. Since there is an imbalance here, Grace "wins" by default. Nancy gives in to her wish, or becomes angry and lashes out; Grace is either overindulged or emotionally injured, and either way, Nancy is deflated and despairing.

Imbalance

Balance is the key. It may seem like an impossible goal or even idea in your present life, but the eleventh step is based on the necessity for and the desire to obtain balance in one's life. When a parent is thrown off balance, she is already defeated, and as Nancy experienced time and again, thrown into despondence: I can't do this right. I can't be a good parent. I can't manage and control my child. It's too hard. I give up.

The good news, as we discussed in the very first chapter, is that you *can't* manage and control your child. You can establish boundaries, you can be consistent in your enforcement of those boundaries, and you can set up consequences if those boundaries are not adhered to. Beyond that, you have little control. Let's digress for a moment and discuss what these boundaries (or the lack thereof) could look like in your family.

Melissa was a career woman, and had remained single until she was almost 40. She married Hunter, a successful businessman, and they both wanted to have a child. A little over a year later, Rachel was born. Hunter encouraged Melissa to stay at home and take care of the baby, since it was not likely that they would have other kids, and they didn't need any additional income for the family.

Rachel was a high-needs baby and a precocious toddler. Melissa rose to the challenge of being a mom to her high-strung daughter. Hunter worked very long hours, brought his laptop home on the weekends to continue his work, and spent very little time with Melissa or Rachel, so the bulk of the parenting work was (and is) Melissa's.

Melissa had little knowledge of boundaries or rules. She had been raised by an overworked mother of three and an alcoholic father from whom she had kept a distance, out of fear of his temper. The "rules" in her home when she was growing up were "stay out of trouble" and "don't aggravate your father." Although she is sometimes lonely for Hunter, she feels that they have a "good marriage" because they don't fight and their home is comparatively peaceful.

When she was younger, Rachel went everywhere with Melissa. They had a very special, close relationship, unhindered by rules or boundaries. When Hunter was away on business, Melissa took Rachel shopping at the mall. She bought her whatever she wanted. Rachel slept in her mother's bed, and they ate at whatever restaurant Rachel desired. Melissa started calling Rachel the "little boss," because she was always telling Melissa what to do. When Melissa was fed up with the "orders," she'd argue with Rachel, lose her temper, and tell her how spoiled she was. Afterward, Melissa felt remorseful and distraught, and she usually made it up to Rachel by taking her out shopping or for ice cream.

When she started school, Rachel began having difficult relationships with new friends. She invited them to her house, and they enjoyed playing with Rachel's toys, but inevitably, they would quarrel about how to play a game, or what clothes they should dress the dolls in. These difficult relationships continued during Rachel's elementary years, as did Melissa's inconsistent parenting style. When her friends got angry with her, Melissa tried to "fix" things for her daughter. She'd arrange elaborate outings for her and her friends that included treats and gifts. If that didn't work, she'd call the friends' moms and set up a tea party or a family event so that the girls would be together. As a final resort, she would fly Rachel away for a long weekend or holiday to Hawaii or a local resort. They would be girlfriends, "just the two of us," as Melissa would say.

"I just don't know what to do with Rachel," Melissa told me on the phone. "She's 13 now and she won't listen to me at all. She argues with me about everything. I got her a cell phone so I could at least keep track of her, and she won't even call me to tell me where she's going after school! She lies about her homework. Her grades are slipping. Whenever I confront her about it, she says she hates it here and wants to go away to boarding school. I couldn't stand that! It's really a mess! I'm so depressed. I miss my little girl. Do you think she'll grow out of this stage?" Melissa had really wanted to keep her daughter a companion and confidante, but as Rachel moved into her adolescence and began to withdraw from her mother, chaos ensued. Both mother and daughter were in distress.

Rachel told me: "My mom is so intrusive. She reads my e-mail and then says she doesn't. She won't let me talk on the phone without finding some excuse to come into my room. She's always finding reasons to 'hang out' with me and my friends when they're around. It's like she thinks she's a teenager. I know this sounds awful, but I just don't really like her. I wish she'd just leave me alone and let me grow up."

Melissa's difficulties are twofold. The first level is

the parenting work she should have done (and hopefully will now begin) about boundaries.

Rules

Family rules are a way of establishing boundaries. Boundaries create safety for kids. When the world of the home reacts the same way, requires the same things, and produces the same results time after time, a child acquires trust in that world. For example, if every time Nancy reaches the checkout stand at the grocery store she says, "I'm not buying any candy," and most importantly, *if she follows through on that decision,* Grace will begin to trust her mother about this one issue. Eventually, Grace can stop testing Nancy about this rule. If Nancy weakens and buys the candy, Grace becomes confused, untrusting, and will then continue to test (and pester) her mother.

In a similar way, Rachel has learned the converse of this rule. She has learned that "every time I have a conflict or a problem, my mother will fix it for me." She has also learned that "the most important thing to my mother is that I like her. I can get away with anything if I threaten to dislike her." This is the antithesis of a boundary. Rachel has learned to manipulate her mother because there have never been any trustworthy, consistent boundaries in their relationship.

A good way to begin establishing boundaries for your children is to decide upon some family rules. These rules must be agreed upon by the parent(s) in the home. If there is only one parent, and the other parent lives in a different home, it will be very helpful to both you and the kids if you can create and maintain the same set of house rules. If there are step-parents and children, it may take some strong determination to set up rules that will work for everyone in the family. Remember that the goal is consistency, so don't draft any laws with which *you* can't follow through.

Here are some examples of house rules:

Garcia Family Rules

1. No hurting others. (This includes: hitting, kicking, biting, name calling, etc.)

2. Everyone uses manners.

3. Everyone has a household responsibility, e.g., taking out the trash, washing dishes, feeding the dog.

4. Respect others' things. (No borrowing without permission.)

5. Everyone returns family phone calls as soon as possible.

6. Everyone cleans up after themselves. This includes:
    - leave bathroom tidy
    - put away food items you take out
    - put your dirty clothes in the hamper

7. Everyone has a bedtime: Ernie, 10 pm, Leticia, 9 pm, Mom and Dad, 11 pm.

8. Everyone takes care of their bodies, including:
    - daily shower and shampoo
    - no alcohol or drug use
    - twice daily teeth brushing

House rules are non-negotiable, and to be respected, they should be universal. In other words, if "no hurting" is our family rule, the kids can't hit each other or the parents, and the parents cannot hit the kids. If mom or dad likes a beer when he or she gets home, "no drinking" would not be a good family rule; instead, "no drinking before age 21" would be appropriate. If you don't want to have a bedtime, "all children have a bedtime" could be substituted.

Family Meeting

The family meeting can be a very useful tool, especially if you're establishing house rules for the first time. Let the kids know that you'll be setting up a new program for your family. Ask them to meet with you at a definite time – for example, Saturday afternoon at 4. You can try posting a bulletin on the front door or refrigerator to help soften the possible resistance to anything new:

Attention Garcia Family!

¡¡ Saturday !!

4pm

– New Family Developments –

Be here to find out whaaas-up!

Mom & Dad

P.S. No excuses – be here on time or else!

It's a good idea to have a short planning meeting with your partner or spouse (if there are two of you) to decide who will present the rules and how the meeting should be run. Remember that these are non-negotiable rules. You don't vote on them together. You just present them to the children. The key is that it's *your* family. You are the ones to decide on the values, morals, and traditions that you want to pass down. The family rules are a means to establish and maintain this framework.

It's helpful, though, if there are some items up for discussion, so the kids can give some input. Perhaps you can be flexible about chores or bedtimes. Wherever you feel you can bend, write that as an "open" rule, e.g., "everyone has chores," and leave it to the family meeting to fill in the specifics. Maybe make a list of possible chores that are age-appropriate for your kids, and allow them to choose from the list. In this way, they have some autonomy in their lives. They need balance in their lives, too.

Consequences

The topic of consequences and discipline could fill (and has filled) a volume. I won't go into great detail here, except to say two important things. Firstly, rules are not really rules if they can't be enforced. If you say, "bedtime is 9 pm," but then do nothing to make sure that Leticia is in bed, she'll disrespect you, disregard the rule, and learn that her family world isn't secure, because there are no real boundaries. This is why a rule that isn't enforced is worse than no rule at all. Secondly, enforcement is an essential part of discipline—punishment is not.

"Punishment is a very ineffective method of discipline…for punishment, strangely enough, often has the effect of teaching the child to behave in exactly the opposite way from the way we want him to behave!"[1] This is because children learn from modeling, as we've discussed previously. What they learn from punishment is "that might makes right. When they are old enough and strong enough, they will try to get their own back, thus many children punish their parents by acting in ways distressing to them."[2]

The root word in "discipline" is "disciple" which, in contrast to how the word is often used, means to teach or train through correction and strengthening. How can a child be strengthened by being humiliated, shamed, emotionally hurt, or physically harmed? She can't. A child needs her parent's consistent help to learn self-discipline. This is accomplished through the family rules in the following manner:

1. House meeting. Establish the rules

2. Explain: house rules are non-negotiable, required for all.

3. Discuss possible consequences for breaking the rules.

4. Follow through.

The consequences for breaking family rules should be discussed by the whole family. Consequences should always be related to the infraction. They should, in effect, be "natural consequences" whenever possible. A parent asked me about this at a meeting one night.

She reported to the parenting group: "We took the family to Grandma's 70th birthday party this weekend, and Stevie (age 4) was looking forward to going all day. He was all dressed up, and everyone was making a bug fuss over him. There was a tray of appetizers on a low table that Stevie was near. Suddenly, he sneezed. Grandma said: 'Stevie— cover your mouth!' Stevie suddenly turned to look at her and, then, with a twinkle in his eyes, made a huge loud *fake* sneeze, directly over the veggie tray! I was horrified! Some of the adults laughed at his prank, but not Grandma. She shook her finger at him and said how 'naughty' he was. He heard her tone of voice and ran out of the room, totally embarrassed. I apologized to Grandma and ran after him. He was crying his eyes out in the other room. What should I have done? I thought I should do something. I didn't know if I should give him a time out or take away a toy—I was just flustered."

Natural consequences! Stevie behaved rudely, Grandma reacted. He received an immediate consequence for his actions. Grandma's scolding had been swift and embarrassing! If Mom had punished him in addition, I don't think Stevie would have received the *benefit* of this embarrassment. No, I don't recommend embarrassing children, but I bet it's a birthday party he'll remember.

At your family meeting, ask for the children's input on fair consequences for various rule breaches; however, be clear that you, the parent, have the final decision. For example, Joanne suggests that a consequence for talking on the phone past bedtime be that she loses her phone privilege for the following day. If this is acceptable, we all agree that this is the consequence. If there is continued abuse of this privilege, you may decide to change the consequences so that Joanne gives up her cell phone for the weekend. If you change the consequences, be sure to inform your daughter of the change, so that she knows what to expect. "Joanne, the consequence for cell phone use after 10 pm has changed. Starting tonight, you can either be off the phone by 10 pm, or give up your phone use for the following weekend. It's your choice." It's very helpful to remind your child that the decision to follow a rule is theirs; it is not a power struggle between you and her, but between her and the rules.

I have found this sentence very helpful: "the rules are set to help you grow up according to the values of our family; therefore, it's my job as your mom to help you learn to abide by them." It's your child's job to struggle with making choices within the limits (rules) you have set. Establish the tone for non-negotiable compliance without attacking a child's character or integrity.

Resist the temptation to say anything else. Especially

with teenagers. Joanne may argue or complain, but you do not need to engage in any further argument about this issue. It is part of the family rules. You can respond to her feelings with "I hear that you're unhappy about my decision," or even "I know it sucks," but don't back down, and don't get drawn into the argument. Sometimes, if your child has gone over the line and is angry about receiving the consequences, you can add, "I know you'll make a different decision next time," or "I'm sure you will choose differently when this comes up again." But only add this if you can say it without sarcasm or rancor. To discipline a child is to strengthen her in her spirit.

Honesty

Let's return to Melissa's problem with Rachel for a minute. While it will be helpful for Melissa to set up family rules and begin to be consistent with her daughter, the underlying dilemma that is really the issue is the misplaced power in their relationship. Melissa is constantly knocked off balance, because she has lost her spiritual ground. This is where the power of the eleventh step lies. Tapping into the spiritual power of this step requires honesty, an open mind, and self-discipline.

This honesty involves the repeated realization that you are powerless over your child and her choices, thoughts and feelings. The only thing you can control is you. Once you have realized this and truly believe it, you are at the surrender that we talked about in the third step. Arriving at this realization now, again, is the deeper surrender that not only have you given up control of your child; you have also given up control of *yourself.*

You have a spirit, and that spirit is running around in your body and mind, trying to live in a physical world. You shortchange yourself every day by not taking advantage of your relationship with your Higher Power.

In order to be spiritually honest, you need to cultivate having an open mind. If you haven't done so yet, you need to take action! Begin by talking with others who have some spiritual base. Read books. Listen to uplifting music. Talk to a mentor or therapist, or journal your feelings about spirituality to help open yourself to the possibilities of the existence of God. Remember that this belief is entirely your own. It does not have to reflect anyone else's understanding or religion. It is *God as you understand Him or Her.*

If a spiritual practice or belief system is not integral to your way of life, it needs to become one; it's a necessary part of these steps. You cannot maintain control over something at the same time that you are actively seeking to "turn your life and will over" to the care of a power greater than yourself. Actively seek God and ask for Him, and He will find you.

The discipline of spirituality also requires continuing action and practice. If you become consistent with yourself in prayer and meditation times, writing and seeking His will, you will find that you have developed the "conscious contact" that this step is talking about. It may present itself as an intuitive thought or a kind of peace that fills you. It may be stronger, and come as pictures or words into your mind as you meditate.

This contact with your Higher Power will provide you with peace, strength, tolerance, and solutions for you and your children. My prayer of choice is always the third step prayer ("I offer my children to thee..."), but the eleventh step has an amazing promise that if I seek His will for myself and my children, I will be given the power to carry it out. I find this to be true both from my experience and others' experiences. If I pray for my children every day, if I maintain the balance and consistency for myself that *I* need, I have a hope and resolve that God will help me provide that balance and consistency for my children as well.

Chapter 10

Seek, and you will find; knock, and the door will be opened wide; ask, you will receive, if you only believe, if you only believe.

~ Bill Worthy

The twelfth step

Having had a spiritual awakening as a result of these steps, I will try to carry this message to others and to practice these principles every day.

Having had a spiritual awakening

The first spiritual experience that I can remember with my children was a shock. Will came home from Mt. Olive Preschool one afternoon and went off to his room to reunite with his toys. From the hallway, I heard him singing cheerfully. It was a simple little song about peanut butter and jelly. It was a new song. I hadn't taught it to him. I didn't even know the words. Here was my precious three-year-old, singing a song I hadn't given to him. He had received a song from a new teacher. I say received, because to me, a song is a gift. I believe God gave us music to soothe our hearts and minds; certainly, there is no organic necessity for music. It doesn't feed, clothe, or shelter us, except perhaps for the shelter it provides us from our own madness at times. But I digress.

Here was my boy, singing. I knew not the words, the

tune, nor the method by which it was taught to him. He had been my own boy, raised, nurtured, and carefully taught by me. I realized with a clarity I had not known before that he truly was one of "God's kids." He was not mine. He did not belong to me. I was not going to teach and protect and mold him forever. He belonged to the world and he belonged to God as *he* (Will) would come to understand Him.

This second part was reinforced several weeks later when we were talking in the kitchen as I prepared lunch for us one day. We had been to church the previous day, as was our usual Sunday routine, and Will had gone to our Sunday school program. It was overseen by a woman named Valinda, who had a kind and gentle spirit. She had been teaching them that morning, and Will reported that the children had been discussing Satan and whether he was real. I replied, noncommittally, that perhaps Satan was that sense or voice inside of us that helps us know right from wrong. Will piped right up and stated with an intensity that chilled me: "Maybe Satan is the voice inside my head that is telling me now not to listen to you." Whoa! Not only does he know his own songs, play his own games and state his own opinions, but he already has a conscious contact: he is already attuned to his conscience. How can this be? He's three!

I began to think back to my own childhood. I remember the feelings I would have in church. I remember wishing I could talk to Jesus and figure out why people acted the way they did; the Sunday school teacher said that we "all love each other" on Sunday, but the Sunday school classmates did not even acknowledge me on Monday in the school hallways. The hypocrisy, hunger and cruelty in the world created doubt in me. But in opposition to that doubt was my own curiosity about the feeling I sometimes had inside me after singing in church next to my father, or the fearful excitement about the power of the thunder and lightning striking a tree just yards from our cabin at Canada Lake, or the magic of the woods right after those storms, when the small red newts would crawl out and sit on top of patches of star moss to soak up the water drops.

How do we reconcile all the misery and iniquities of the world with the supremacy and spectacle of God's nature? How do we understand that cruelty and love coexist in a world that a benevolent God created? To a developing child, these are impossible questions. To adolescents, this is cause for rebellion and declarations that God doesn't care, or even worse, that He never was: that we are here alone, flukes of an evolutional growth spurt with no purpose, meaning or destiny. It is not my intent in this work to dispute the merits or foundations of religion. It is not pertinent to parenting that you find or adhere to any specific religious belief system. I believe, however, that it is imperative to attain and maintain some form of a spiritual connection with a Power greater than you.

This Power will help you let go of your toddler's hand so that he can learn to climb up the ladder and go down the slide by himself. It will support you while you walk your 5-year-old to school for the first time and place his malleable mind into the teaching hands of a complete stranger. It will comfort you as you allow your lovely, impressionable, 12-year-old daughter to go with some friends to the mall by herself. It will guide you in establishing what is right and fair and respectful for your family. Most of all, as a parent, this Power will be the One to whom you can surrender your fears, doubts, worries, and best intentions.

I will carry this message to others

It will be helpful, perhaps, to carry this message to other parents. I encourage you to do that. Seek out those parents who are unsure, confused, angry and distraught. Tell them that you have found a better way. Offer them comfort in this, the spiritual solution. Share your experience of surrender, house cleaning, and seeking God, and if you have found peace as a result, tell them that this has been the solution for you.

There is another and perhaps more important way to "carry this message," and that is through us to our children. What do you imagine happens when you tell an anguished teen that you understand that he really wants to have a car and you will "pray about" it? Or if, instead of punishing your tantrumming child, you hold him firmly in your arms, repeating: "I'm going to help you control your body until you can control yourself?"

There was an incident, many years ago, when Will was about six and James about three. I had been away for the afternoon, and when I returned I was met at the door by a distraught sitter and an anxious boy. The house was in a jumble, and I was immediately thrown into some form of distress. The sitter tried to talk, but Will moved right in front of her and demanded my attention. Our conversation began thus:

"Will, you look upset!"

"I am, Mommy. Look." He held out his shaky pale fist and, as he opened it, revealed a small bunch of hair. It was not shorn hair; it was pulled, and, by the looks, a good-sized hunk, maybe an eighth of an inch in diameter.

"Oooohh," I exclaimed with a worried voice and an upset face. "What happened?"

"I pulled Jamie's hair," he immediately confessed, tears beginning to well up.

"Ouch. That must've hurt." I looked at Jamie, who was half smiling and looking inquisitively from Will to me and back again. Will then rolled up his sleeve to expose a fresh red bite mark on his shoulder. I wilted inside. My poor, upset boys. I felt so many things: sad, scared, angry, curious. Fortunately, I had the composure to wait.

"Oh, no!" I exclaimed again, with measured concern. "Man, you two must've had a bad fight." Will nodded and Jamie, remembering now that he too was injured, rubbed his head and began to look upset. I thought quickly. I was distraught, not so much at their fighting or breaking family rules, but at the obvious pain that Will was in, thinking of the injury he'd done to his brother. I could see it so clearly on his face. He began to ask me in a trembling voice, what his "consequences" were. I looked from one to the other. I got down on my knees to look into Will's troubled spirit. I could see it breaking in half. God came to my rescue and gave me the words.

"Will," I began gently, "I think you've already paid your 'consequences.'" He looked puzzled. "How do you feel inside?"

"Bad," was all he could get out before the tears tumbled down his cheeks.

"I know. It doesn't feel good when you hurt someone else, does it?"

"No." Snuffles. "So what should be my consequences?"

"I think that feeling inside of you is your consequence." I waited a moment for him to take this in. "And when I feel bad because I've done something wrong, the first thing I do is tell God I'm sorry. Then I tell the other person I'm sorry. And I try to make it up to the person."

"OK." He went over to Jamie and hugged him and said he was sorry. Jamie said the same thing; whether or not he got what was going on is still a mystery. But one thing is certain. It was the power and the grace of God that helped me avoid compounding the damage done to either child.

Had I reacted in anger to the evident turmoil when I first arrived home, the whole lesson would have been lost. Because God gave me the grace to "pause when agitated,"[1] I was able to help my child learn from the situation. He was able to sense what his true feelings were (guilt, sadness, hurt), and he learned how to make amends to someone. And I was able to see in a concrete way that in order to parent, I do not have to be in control—leading, organizing, lecturing—to make sure that my children get the lesson the way I think they should. I can help my children learn by standing next to them.

Timing

The idea that children need to learn in their own way and in their own time is stated succinctly by Bruno Bettleheim, noted child psychologist, who says:

> This shows the importance of keeping in mind that a child can see things only in his own frame of reference, which is very different from ours. If we remain aware of this simple fact—although what may be involved in our intercourse with each other may be very complex—then all will be well. We will see our child and his problems clearly—not through a glass darkened or distorted by our self-involvement, by our emotional involvement in our past, or our anxieties about the future.[2]

I'm reminded of a dad and son that I witnessed eating ice cream together on a balmy summer evening. They were sitting outside at a small table, and Riley, a boy of about 4 years or so, was sitting with his dad, enjoying his treat. Suddenly, another child of a slightly younger age came running out of the ice cream parlor, mother trailing behind, calling to him frantically: "Dewayne! Dewayne! Stop!" Dewayne, full of ice cream and energy, obviously did not have ears for his mother's warnings, and ran directly across the parking lot. A car stopped suddenly to avoid hitting the boy, and all eyes in the vicinity were on the mother and child as she caught up to him, grabbed him up in her arms, and scolded him severely.

Meanwhile, Riley's dad began to pester: "Riley. Do you see that?" Riley was deep into his chocolate and didn't even look up. "Riley. Riley!" Riley looked up briefly, then back at his spoon. "Riley, don't you *ever* run into a parking lot like that! Riley—do you hear me?" Riley didn't. Father repeated. "Riley—" he moved his head down to Riley's eye level, so his son would be forced to acknowledge his petition. "Never run into parking lots!" He glanced up at Dad. "K," he mumbled, slurping down the last of his dessert.

Children are in a state of being. We are not. They are in the moment. We are in the past, feeling bad about what we've done or fantasizing about how wonderful it was—or we're in the future, worrying about how our child might be killed in a parking lot accident or dreaming about him becoming a star quarterback. When our moments are not child-centered, we're thinking about how we forgot to go to the bank to make our deposit, or how we really need to put gas in the car before we drive downtown to the office tomorrow morning. Our moments are lost to the worries and fears, plans and fantasies of adult reality. Most of us who become parents have lost the art of momentary awareness. Riley's relationship with his dad would have benefited more by his observation of Riley's enjoyment of the moment. He could have said: "mmmm, that's good ice cream, eh?" and at least he would have been present with his son in his moment. Later, perhaps when they were driving home, he could have found a moment to teach Riley about parking lot safety.

The problem is that, as parents, we are so worried that we'll miss an opportunity to teach our child, show our child, help our child grow up into a healthy, responsible, able adult that we forget entirely to enjoy their childishness. Learning is something that only happens when the student is ready. Teaching is an art form of timing. The ability to be spontaneous, to let go of control, and to surrender to what God wants from you at this very moment is the essence of living a spirit-filled life.

Since timing is everything, teaching your child about her spirituality cannot be agenda-driven; it must be natural and interesting to her. Follow her curiosity, ask her what she thinks, pray for her and with her when she's ready. As you pray and meditate and learn from your Higher Power, you will develop the strength and self-awareness to be a spiritual guide to her. I began praying every night for my children when they were quite young. It was a routine that became expected. I always asked them what they wanted me to pray for, and what their concerns from their day were. Often, they did not know or respond, and I would simply pray for good dreams, peace, and rest for their bodies, minds and spirits. If we had difficulty during the day and I sensed there was still some anger or frustration, I would pray about that, always being careful not to blame them or include criticism. If they were worried about their pets or their friends, I would pray for them. I prayed conversationally, not by rote or dogma. I prayed to God as I understood Him, asking for knowledge of His will for us and the power to carry that out. I was teaching them by example that I lean on God and that they can, too.

This portion of the twelfth step has been the greatest reward of my parenting journey thus far. When Will lost his hamster in the house, we all prayed for it to be found. When Jamie had surgery as a 2-year-old, we all prayed for his recovery. When our grandpa passed away recently, we all huddled together, arms linked, and prayed for strength for Grandma, peace for Grandpa's soul, and comfort for the whole family. We all cried together. When we have family meetings about quarrels or new rules, we pray before we begin that God will protect all of our feelings and keep us from hurting each other. When we're done, we thank Him for His help. All of these actions are teaching our children every day. We do not have to control or arrange spiritual teaching; it comes as an organic part of our practicing the twelfth step in every area of our lives.

As you begin this 12-step process with your children and yourself, it may feel awkward and uncomfortable. I can assure you, from experience, that it will change, and you will grow as you humble yourself, admit your flaws, and seek guidance from the greatest Parent of all. "A Vision for You,"

from the book *Alcoholics Anonymous,* is my favorite
reminder of this fact.

A vision for you

Our book is meant to be suggestive only. We
realize we know only a little. God will
constantly disclose more to you and to us.
Ask Him in your morning meditation what
you can do each day...The answers will
come, if your house is in order. But obviously
you cannot transmit something you haven't
got. See to it that your relationship with Him
is right, and great events will come to pass...

Abandon yourself to God as you understand
God. Admit your faults to Him and to your
fellows. Clear away the wreckage of your
past. Give freely of what you find and join us.
We shall be with you in the Fellowship of the
Spirit, and you will surely meet some of us as
you trudge the Road of Happy Destiny.[3]

Afterword

It is my sincere hope that you will follow these Twelve Steps to the precise extent that they speak to your life and resonate with your inner experience as a parent. Let the steps minister to you, your sad, tired injuries, your imperfections and flaws, and your desires to do the best for your children. Through their God-given power, may they guide you, teach you, comfort you and strengthen you, and because of that, quiet your fears and bring peace, love, and respect to your children. My prayer for you and your children is that you receive the serenity resulting from surrender, the freedom to engage in the struggle for growth, and liberty from the bondage of perfection.

Appendix ~ Suggested worksheets for the steps

The first step

I am powerless over my child and his or her life is unmanageable by me.

On the form below, list examples of your powerlessness over your child. If you have more than one child, copy this page and do the exercise two times, inserting each child's name. If you use up all of the spaces on this page, use extra paper as needed. As an example, you might write: "I am powerless over Wendy and her mood swings."

I am powerless over

_____

_____

_____

_____

_____

_____

_____

_____

_____

_____

The first step

I am powerless over my child and his or her life is unmanageable by me.

In the second half of the first step, list the ways in which your child's life is unmanageable by you. This may include examples of unmanageability in your own life as well, as pertaining to your child.

For example: My life is unmanageable; I have insomnia because I'm worrying about Wendy's choice of friends. Another example: Wendy's life is unmanageable by me; she picks friends who aren't loyal, and they upset her.

_____

_____

_____

_____

_____

_____

_____

_____

_____

_____

The second step

I am willing to believe that a power greater than myself can restore me to sanity.

This step requires thought, prayer and meditation. If you have a spiritual belief in place already, this is the time to press in. Seek guidance. Ask for restoration. Pray for the willingness to be teachable, so that you can find your way through the next ten steps.

If you are in doubt, confusion, or disbelief that there is "One Who Has All Power,"[1] it's time to do some searching. This step doesn't require that you belong to a religious sect or organization. It doesn't mandate a profound belief system. It only suggests that you be willing to believe in a power greater than you, and in turn, to seek to know that power so that you can be restored. Here are a few suggestions if you are struggling with seeking and finding:

1. Talk to people you admire, especially people who seem to "have it all together." Ask them how they handle the stressors of raising children, working, maintaining a home, scheduling events, spending time with partners or spouses, and cleaning the house. Ask if they have a faith that works for them.

2. Question people you know who belong to a church, temple or other religious organization. If their group sparks interest in you, ask to go with them. When you go, shake people's hands and ask them questions.

3. Find spiritual books, articles, tapes, and CDs. Read, absorb, and listen with an open mind, spirit, and heart.

4. Find a quiet place that is soothing to your senses. Write down your concerns, worries, and wishes for your children. Sit quietly and ask for God to help you. You may be surprised to find that He shows up.

The third step

I am decided to turn my child's life and will over to the care of God, *as I understand Him.*

This step is a writing step. Once you feel you have completed the second step and are at least becoming familiar with the idea of God, it's time to figure out how to surrender your child. This step may be the most difficult for some (I know it was for me), and it will be very helpful if you know someone with whom to share it. Start by reviewing your lists of powerlessness and unmanageability. In whatever style suits you, write all of the things about this child that you need to surrender or "turn over" to your HP. For example:

I'm so angry and frustrated by Wendy! I'm powerless over her mood swings and the fact that she gets upset every time she talks to her boyfriend. I wish she would just break up with him. He's no good for her. I want her to scream at him, but that's what she's doing to her sisters all the time. Please, God, help me to let go of her moods. I'm powerless over all of her choices.

This writing could also be abbreviated, if you wish: *I'm turning Wendy's friends, boyfriend, moods and whole life over to you, God!* As noted earlier, simply substituting your child's name into the Third Step Prayer and repeating it daily is a sound spiritual and parenting practice.

> God, I offer <u>Wendy</u> to You,
> To build with <u>her</u> and do with her what You will.
> Relieve <u>Wendy</u> of the bondage of self,
> That <u>she</u> may better do Your will.
> Take away <u>her</u> difficulties, that victory over them
> May bear witness to those <u>she</u> would help
> Of Your Power, Your Love, and Your Way of Life.
> May <u>Wendy</u> do Your will always.

The fourth step

I am willing to make a searching and fearless moral inventory of myself.

This is the most labor-intensive step. It is also emotionally intense due to the excavating that it requires. Begin with soul-searching to identify the areas in your past that affected you strongly and that have impact on any emotional, mental, and spiritual interactions with your child. I suggest writing only the negative or harmful things that still shadow your consciousness. These are the things that you are most likely to carry into your parenting. The inventory should include at least three main areas: resentments, fears, and hurts. Use a long handwritten form, or something like this as a suggested format:

I'm angry at:	Incident:	My response:	Affects my:	My part:
Wendy	She snuck out of the house at night	screamed at her irrationally	self-esteem peace	I wasn't firm with rules

I'm hurt by:	Incident:	My response:	Affects my:	My part:

The sixth step

I am now ready to ask my Higher Power to reveal and remove all of my character flaws.

This is a simple list-making step. Most likely, you have all of the character defects, at least in some measure. Write them all as they are revealed to you through your now-completed inventory, or through prayer.

My Character Flaws:

_____

_____

_____

_____

_____

_____

_____

_____

_____

_____

_____

_____

The eighth step

I am willing to have my Higher Power reveal to me anyone I have harmed.

Quiet, reflective prayer will reveal to you the faces of those you have harmed. List these persons below, along with anyone from your inventory to whom you owe amends. If there are those who would be hurt by confessing old betrayals or injuries, it is best to handle these emotional debts with your Higher Power or a friend or sponsor. Do not reap your freedom from the past by hurting another.

Ex: I owe Dad money – I dented his car and never paid him

The ninth step

I'm willing to make amends to whomever I have hurt.

As before, be certain before making amends that you won't cause harm to the one receiving it. Also, consider whether the person (in the case of a child, especially) is capable of understanding the amends. If it is an incident that happened so long ago and was specific only to your feelings, it may be that the child or other person will not benefit at all from this transaction. In this case, it's probably best, if it is not severely disabling to your parenting work, to allow your HP to take it on so that you can let it go.

Here is a sample of an amends letter:

Dear Mom,

I'm writing to let you know that I'm sorry I was such a dreadful teenager. Now that Sandi is 14 and "boy crazy," I'm beginning to see just how hard your job was! Please forgive me for any worry, fear and anxiety I caused you during those years.

Your loving daughter

It's not necessary (or advisable) to add: "in seventh grade, I smoked pot for the first time; in tenth grade, I got pregnant and didn't tell you about the abortion; and when I went away to college, I robbed a 7-Eleven!" Your mom doesn't need to know the sordid details of your bad behavior. If you have a need to confess these beyond the reading of your fourth step, find a spiritual guide and work on it privately.

The most important part in any amends letter is to avoid justifying or rationalizing your behavior. Remember that this is *your* work. You are making amends so that your slate will be wiped clean. Carefully consider each amends so that you don't have underlying expectations.

The tenth step

I will continue to take daily inventory, and when I'm wrong, promptly admit it.

Here is a suggested format for your Daily Inventory:

When have I acted out in anger?

_____

_____

_____

When have I held onto resentment?

_____

_____

_____

When was I dishonest?

_____

_____

_____

When was I selfish?

_____

_____

_____

When have I been fearful?

_____

_____

_____

In *Alcoholics Anonymous*, the authors state that fear "ought to be classed with stealing. It seems to cause more trouble."[2] Indeed, if you begin to list your fears every day, you will see how your life is ruled by them. I catch myself dozens of times a day feeling fearful that Will is not safe while he's driving, or that James will not be safe outside in our own driveway shooting baskets, that my husband won't make it home from work, that a stranger I see in the elevator wants to take me hostage...you get the idea.

I remember walking Will in the stroller when he was only about 2 months old. I was with my friend, Krista, who had her 8-month-old son in a stroller also. Across the park, about 100 yards from us, were two men, talking and walking together. I sheepishly asked Krista, "did you ever think that those two men might come across the park, threaten us with guns, and steal our babies from us?" I snickered a bit, to throw her off track, but she instantly replied, "oh, all the time!" We laughed at ourselves and our mother-anxiety spilling out in living, fearful color.

We live in a culture and a time when the media, the entertainment, even the language is saturated with fear. We are attacked daily with stories of drive-by shootings, drug overdoses, child molestations. Everyone you know locks their doors, tells you to "be careful" when you drive off in your car, and warns you of impending natural disasters. Add to that the physical, emotional, and instinctual attachment that you have with your children. How could we not be fearful? This is precisely why the first three steps are so arduous. It is also precisely why we need to practice them daily! List your fears on paper. See them when they crop up in your thoughts during your day, hear them in your voice when you warn your children, and then ask God to take them from you, because, no matter what your mind tells you, they offer you no help, support, or advantage in actually keeping your children safe. All they do is steal from you. Fear steals your time, emotional energy, and peace. Don't let it!

In dealing with fear—indeed, in all of my emotionally charged reactions that affect my children—I try to always keep in mind the comforting wisdom of the Alchoholics Anonymous Big Book:

Without help it is too much for us.

But there is One who has all power—that One is God.

May you find Him now! [3]

Notes

Part I

Heading quotation: Gibran, Kahlil (1971).

Chapter 1

Heading quotation: Ginott, Haim G. (1965).

1. Ginott, Haim G. (1965).

Chapter 2

Heading quotation: Franklin, Benjamin

1. Alcoholics Anonymous World Services, inc. (1976).
2. Alcoholics Anonymous World Services, inc. (1976).
3. Alcoholics Anonymous World Services, inc. (1976).
4. Bartleby, John, 1919.

Chapter 3

Heading quotation: Faber, Adele, & Mazlilsh, Elaine (1980).

1. Bettleheim, Bruno, (1987).
2. Winnicott, D.W. (1987).
3. Winnicott, D.W. (1994).
4. Ginott, Haim G. (1965).
5. Alcoholics Anonymous World Services, inc. (1976).

Part II

Heading quotation: Bettleheim, Bruno, (1987).

Chapter 4

Heading quotation: Bettleheim, Bruno, (1987).

1. Alcoholics Anonymous World Services, inc. (1976).
2. Miller, Alice (1983).
3. Miller, Alice (1983).
4. Alcoholics Anonymous World Services, inc. (1976).
5. Miller, Alice (1983).
6. Miller, Alice (1983).

Chapter 5

Heading quotation: Miller, Alice (1983).

1. Alcoholics Anonymous World Services, inc. (1976).
2. Alcoholics Anonymous World Services, inc. (1976).
3. Gospel Communications International (2005).
4. Alcoholics Anonymous World Services, inc. (1976).

Chapter 6

Heading quotation: Prager, Dennis (2006).

1. Alcoholics Anonymous World Services, inc. (1976).

Part III

Heading quotation: Spencer, Herbert

Chapter 7

Heading quotation: Alcoholics Anonymous World Services, inc. (1976)

1. Arterburn, Stephen, & Stokers, Fred (2003).
2. Bowlby, John (1979).

3. American Psychiatric Association (1994).

4. Bowlby, John (1979).

5. Wikimedia Foundation (2001).

Chapter 8

Heading quotation: Gospel Communications International (2005).

1. Faber, Adele, & Mazlilsh, Elaine (1980).

Chapter 9

Heading quotation: Alcoholics Anonymous World Services, inc. (1976).

1. Dodson, Fitzhugh, (1977).

2. Bettleheim, Bruno, (1987).

Chapter 10

Heading quotation: Worthy, Bill, (1993) from Matthew 7:7.

2. Alcoholics Anonymous World Services, inc. (1976).

3. Bettleheim, Bruno, (1987).

4. Alcoholics Anonymous World Services, inc. (1976).

Appendix

1. Alcoholics Anonymous World Services, inc. (1976).

2. Alcoholics Anonymous World Services, inc. (1976).

3. Alcoholics Anonymous World Services, inc. (1976).

Bibliography

Alcoholics Anonymous World Services, inc. (1976). *Alcoholics anonymous* (3rd ed.). New York: Alcoholics Anonymous World Services, inc. (Original work published in 1953)

> *Twelve steps and twelve traditions* (1981). New York: Alcoholics Anonymous World Services, inc. (Original work published in 1939)

American Psychiatric Association, (1994). *Diagnostic and statistical manual of mental disorders* (4th ed.) Washington DC: American Psychiatric Association.

Arterburn, Stephen, & Stoeker, Fred (2003). *Preparing your son for every man's battle.* Colorado Springs, CO: WaterBrook Press

BibleGateway.com, *Philippians* 4:6-8 [Electronic version] Gospel Communications International (2005). Retrieved March, 2005, from Bartleby.com *John* 12:36, [Electronic version] Gospel Communications International (2005). Retrieved March, 2005, from BibleGateway.com

Bartleby, John, *Familiar Quotations 10th Edition*, comp, 1919. [Electronic version] Retrieved March, 2005, from Bartleby.com

Bettleheim, Bruno, (1987). *A good enough parent.* New York: Vintage Books.

Bowlby, John, (1988). *A secure base: Parent-child attachment and healthy human development*, New York: Basic Books.

The making and breaking of affectional bonds (1979). New York: Routledge

Dodson, Fitzhugh, (1977). How to discipline with love (from crib to college). New York: Signet.

Faber, Adele, & Mazlilsh, Elaine (1980). *How to talk so kids will listen and listen so kids will talk.* New York: Avon Books.

Liberated parents, liberated children - Your guide to a happier family (1990). New York: Avon Books.

Gibran, Kahlil (1971). *The prophet.* New York: Alfred A. Knopf. (Original work published in 1923)

Ginott, Haim G. (1965). *Between parent and child.* New York: Three Rivers Press.

Miller, Alice (1983). *For your own good.* (3rd ed.). (Hildegarde & Hunter Hannum, Trans.) New York: Noonday Press. (Original work published in 1980)

Wikipedia.org, Prayer of St. Francis of Assisi [Electronic version] Wikimedia Foundation (2001). Retrieved March, 2005, from Wikipedia.org

Winnicott, D.W. (1987). *The child, the family, and the outside world.* USA: Perseus Publishing. (Original work published in 1964.)

Playing and reality. (1994). London: Tavistock Publications Ltd. (Original work published in 1971.)